A Road of Unimagined Adventure

PRAISE FOR
A ROAD OF UNIMAGINED ADVENTURE

"Most stories, especially self-made ones, are thin and bland. But occasionally there are human stories that are made thick and compelling by a speaking God and a listening person. This is the case with Kevin Springer as told in *A Road of Unimagined Adventure*. Any parent, leader, or spiritual seeker will grow from Kevin's experience of hearing God's Big Words."

-Todd Hunter, Anglican bishop, author of
Deep Peace: Finding Calm in a World of Conflict and Anxiety

"Never has a generation of pastors and leaders needed a book such as this. Kevin Springer has distilled for us the one thing we need so desperately and want so deeply—to hear the voice of God so that we can experience the adventure of his intentions for us. The advent of pervasive digital slavery has stuffed our collective spiritual ears with cultural cotton and useless investments of our precious energy. This book is a prophetic tale and Spirit-led 'ear-echtomy' for those of us who believe but are not personally experiencing the promise of knowing and hearing the voice of Jesus."

-Kenny Luck, founder of Every Man Ministries,
former pastor of men and teaching pastor at Saddleback Church,
and an ECPA Platinum Award-winning author of over thirty books

"Kevin Springer's book, *A Road of Unimagined Adventure*, is long overdue. In it, he details the story of his own life, marked by Big Words, given at specific moments where God spoke to him and to his wife, directing them at key inflection points. Many people—including Christians—struggle with the idea of God speaking today, and many more struggle with actually hearing Him when He does speak. Kevin shows us how he discerned the voice of God when Big Words came. While he does not flinch from the reality of the supernatural, neither does he cheapen these divine moments with fanciful stories. He also shows the agony and the ecstasy of the failures and successes of life, thereby helping the reader to see how listening to God, particularly at those key crossroads moments, leads to an incredible life-long adventure with God. This book will make you desire and help you have your own adventure."

-**Ken Fish,** founder, Orbis Ministries, Falls Church, VA.
B.A. (Princeton University),
M.Div. (Fuller Theological Seminary), MBA (UCLA)

A Road of Unimagined Adventure is a great memoir of candid personal life lessons and reflections by Kevin Springer. It will inspire and encourage those considering the meaning of their lives: those just beginning their journey with the Lord as well as those who have been walking with him for a long time. A very enjoyable and an inspiring read for all."

-**Dave Nodar**, founder and senior leader, ChristLife,
Catholic Ministry for Evangelization, Baltimore, MD

"Kevin Springer is a friend and mentor of mine. *A Road of Unimagined Adventure* had me in tears by the third page. As a US Navy Chaplain, my life has been shaped by discerning Big Words from the Lord. As I share these stories with marines and sailors in conversations and counseling sessions around the world, they continue to minister directly to weary hearts, and point us all back to the loving arms of our dear Savior. This is a must-read for every Christ-follower."

-Lt. Brandon Kenyon, chaplain, US Navy

"Kevin Springer is a walking treasure trove of Vineyard history, and his honest and humble recounting of his relationship with John Wimber and the early Vineyard days is a great way to get to know our spiritual predecessors. Kevin's dedication to following the Big Words he received from the Lord is a beautiful example of faithfulness, with trust and obedience marking his story from start to finish. *A Road of Unimagined Adventure* is a gift to the church, specifically to pastors, as his transparency about some of the more difficult dynamics in church-planting and leadership will help pastors to feel seen and encouraged to continue pressing forward."

-Jay Pathak, national director, Vineyard USA

"Kevin Noble Springer's *A Road of Unimagined Adventure* is a true story of an extraordinary couple who have been led in their lives by what they call 'Big Words from God.' It is a one in a thousand book that will both challenge and inspire you as you read it."

-Paul Cedar, former chairman/CEO of
The Mission America Coalition (now The Table Coalition),
and president of the Evangelical Free Church of America

"I was recently asked to design a course for emerging leaders in Ethiopia and have just found the textbook: *A Road of Unimagined Adventure*. The purpose of the course is to equip leaders to multiply movements that reach people for Christ, make disciples, develop leaders, and reproduce churches. It's all here in Kevin Noble Springer's book—not in theory but lived out fruitfully and faithfully over a lifetime, together with his wife of over 50 years, Suzanne. ...I resonated with their journey on a deep emotional level, choking up fifteen to twenty times while reading. Kevin and I both have lived 'unimagined adventures' because of the Big Words God imparted to us . . . What character traits guided Kevin and Suzanne to finish well? So many men and women start out strong only to end up washing out in ministry and marriage. Why didn't Kevin and Suzanne? Read. You won't be disappointed."

-**Linus John Morris**, B.S., M.Div., and D.Min. in Transformational Leadership, former president and co-founder of Christian Associates, current missional catalyst for Global Training Network

A ROAD OF UNIMAGINED ADVENTURE

a memoir

*How Big Words
Have Shaped My Life*

KEVIN NOBLE SPRINGER

NASHVILLE

NEW YORK • LONDON • MELBOURNE • VANCOUVER

A Road of Unimagined Adventure

How Big Words Have Shaped My Life

Published in New York, New York, by Morgan James Publishing. Morgan James is a trademark of Morgan James, LLC. www.MorganJamesPublishing.com

Proudly distributed by Publishers Group West®

Morgan James BOGO™

A **FREE** ebook edition is available for you or a friend with the purchase of this print book.

CLEARLY SIGN YOUR NAME ABOVE

Instructions to claim your free ebook edition:
1. Visit MorganJamesBOGO.com
2. Sign your name CLEARLY in the space above
3. Complete the form and submit a photo of this entire page
4. You or your friend can download the ebook to your preferred device

ISBN 9781636981789 paperback
ISBN 9781636981796 ebook
Library of Congress Control Number:
2023934471

Cover Design by:
Rachel Lopez
www.r2cdesign.com

Interior Design by:
Christopher Kirk
www.GFSstudio.com

Editing by:
Kevin Perrotta
Ann Arbor, Michigan

Morgan James PUBLISHING

Builds

with...
Habitat for Humanity®
Peninsula and
Greater Williamsburg

Morgan James is a proud partner of Habitat for Humanity Peninsula and Greater Williamsburg. Partners in building since 2006.

Get involved today! Visit: www.morgan-james-publishing.com/giving-back

For

Suzanne

"Rejoice in the wife of your youth,
A lovely deer, a graceful doe."
Proverbs 5:18–19

Suzanne Nadal and Kevin Springer, age five

TABLE OF CONTENTS

ACKNOWLEDGMENTS

I want to start by thanking my wife, Suzanne, who never tired of reading endless revisions and who contributed insights and anecdotes that breathed life into our journey. When I wearied of yet another rewrite, she reminded me of Jack London's observation that "it takes hard writing to make easy reading." Nobody has the insight into this journey that Suzanne has, because we are living it together. This is *our* story, and for that I thank God every day.

The first draft was read by Bert Ghezzi, a seasoned editor and writer who forty years ago recommended me to my first editorial position at Servant Publications in Ann Arbor, Michigan. Bert's insights into writing memoirs helped me immensely.

Kevin Perrotta, my writing mentor, and the editor of books that I wrote with John Wimber, was once again willing to coach me and tirelessly edit every page. His comments, corrections, and insights improved each chapter. Thank you and your wife Louise for being true friends.

Carol Wimber-Wong was particularly encouraging, and her Foreword fills in critical background to chapters seven and eight. Carol lived a magnificent journey with her husband, John

Wimber. Her journey continues today with her husband Ken. They had a profound impact on Suzanne and me and so many others. Thank you, Carol.

Joel Kilpatrick, an accomplished writer of many books, has encouraged me through the ups and downs of writing an intimate book. Shortly before I started this book he and I met at my granddaughter's and his daughter's soccer tournament in Temecula, California. Joel lives nearby, so we were able to meet regularly through the Covid restrictions. We are now friends for life.

I'm also grateful for Judy Nichols (Mansfield, Ohio), Pastor Jack Bailey (Redlands, California), Linda Caruso (San Pedro, California), Pastor Dave Dove (Salinas, California), my Pastor David Deutsch, Jeffrey Tyner (Redding, California), US Navy Chaplain Brandon Kenyon, Pastor Keith and Cid Newsome (Denison, Texas), and Maggie LePley (Ballard, California), who took the time to read early drafts and offer insights, corrections, and encouragement that made the book more complete. Tom Colivas (Camarillo) and I met weekly to discuss each chapter. Psychologist Becky Branch (Temecula, California) provided insights into my mother's complicated and traumatic childhood and how it affected her and me. My cousin, Marilee Moore (Keizer, Oregon), contributed historical background of my paternal grandparents, including my grandmother's memoir. Each person comes from a different era of my life, knowing me in different capacities and geographic locations.

Neal Parrow, my son-in-law and a gifted artist/illustrator, worked many hours breathing new life into tired, old photographs that make them pop off the pages. Neal's creative cover and book suggestions were invaluable.

There are two people who deserve special recognition for their contribution to my journey. The first is Ray Nethery, my mentor of over fifty years with whom I talk almost weekly. At age 93 he is as vibrant and insightful as ever! Secondly, Milt McKenzie's support and loyal friendship for thirty years have modeled biblical generosity and integrity. God used you to change Suzanne's and my life, Milt, and we thank God every day for you.

A memoir is incomplete without insights into your family, so I am particularly grateful for our children taking the time to read and comment on their dad's story. Thank you, Kelley Parrow (husband Neal), Shad Springer (wife Maggie Yates), and Alyssa West (husband David). This book was written for you and our grandchildren—Annie, J.D., Micah, Titus, and Benjamin. Our journey is your heritage. I love you.

Kevin Noble Springer
Camarillo, California

FOREWORD

Long before John and I met Kevin Springer, we were praying for him. We had received a word from God—what Kevin calls a "Big Word" in *A Road of Unimagined Adventure*—that we would immediately recognize the person who would write books with John.

For several years John had received multi-book offers from publishers on the topics of signs and wonders, evangelism, and healing. Though John was a pastor, speaker, and musician, he had neither the time nor background to write books without the aid of a writer who understood his heart, values, and vision.

John needed help from a person he trusted and who was able to capture his words and pass them along to readers all over the world. So we prayed. For more than three years. And then one day an editor from Ann Arbor, Michigan, called John and requested an interview. The interview went well. We discovered that like us, Kevin was a Californian, pastor, and a risk taker. He also had a broad background working with a variety of denominations, from Roman Catholic and Episcopalian to Presbyterian and Baptist. There was an obvious connection between John and Kevin. John wondered, "Could this be the writer?"

When the interview was published, John and I knew Kevin was the one we had been praying for. John said, "He captured my voice! Finally, someone gets me." However, we needed to do our due diligence, first inviting Kevin to a conference in Houston, then out to California to spend time with us and other key members of the Vineyard family. Upon meeting his wife, Suzanne, we learned they are a team—she is an editor. The Holy Spirit said, "Sign the book contracts with Kevin."

John and I were looking for a writer, but we got more—new friends with the same hunger for God as we had.

Kevin's memoirs capture what John and I discovered is the secret of life: Love Christ with all your heart, all your mind, and all your soul. Then cultivate listening to his voice and obeying when he speaks, putting him first in everything you do. And then get ready for the ride of your life!

Who is this book written for? Though anyone can profit from reading *A Road of Unimagined Adventure*, because Kevin is reflecting on his experiences as a leader, this is for leaders seeking the keys to making wise decisions and how to navigate the unpredictable results. Kevin doesn't sugar-coat his journey, but always leaves the reader with hope and confidence in God's presence, power, and provision to complete any task he calls you to.

There's a second group of people who would benefit from this story: married couples. This is Kevin *and* Suzanne's story, thoughts on how formidable events impacted their marriage. What I find most encouraging is the portrait of a husband-and-wife whose uncompromising commitment to God in some of the most trying circumstances deepened their love for one another. The Springers offer hope to all marriages that this path can be for them too.

I am confident you will love Kevin and Suzanne's unimagined adventure as much as I do.

Carol Wimber-Wong is the widow of John Wimber and author of *The Way it Was*. Carol and her husband Ken live in Yorba Linda, California.

INTRODUCTION

The Garage

Camarillo, California

When the Apostle Paul was detained by the Emperor Nero in Rome in AD 60, he had to wonder what God was doing. For the next two years he was under house arrest, but he continued ministering to visitors and encouraging churches through letters.

God grounded Paul, a consummate Type-A activist, compelling him to sit down and write. Paul's four "Prison Letters" (also called epistles) were written during that period. They include letters to the Ephesians, Philippians, Colossians, and a little letter to Philemon—four of the most translated and influential letters in the history of the world. What Nero meant for evil, God used to advance his Gospel to the entire world, up to today.

I'm no Paul, but I identify with him. I too have a Type-A personality. And I love starting things—ministries, magazines, books—to meet new challenges and influence people to live for God.

My own activism came to an abrupt halt in March of 2020 when California went on COVID-19 pandemic lockdown. I sheltered in place, turning our guest house into an office, feeling like God put me under house arrest.

For my wife Suzanne, though, this was an opportunity to clean out our garage and sort through over fifty years of marriage and childhood memorabilia. The quarantine was a strange answer to her prayers for time. For more than a year she had been discipled online by Joshua Becker, the guru of minimalism, and this was her chance for us to conquer our Mt. Everest of accumulated history. She loved to say, "We can't leave this mess to our children when we die. Besides, their heritage is in these boxes."

Groaning as I looked around the garage, I knew I was cornered.

I volunteered to sort through 38 legal boxes stuffed with photographs. Suzanne tackled the numerous document and "sentimental" boxes.

You could say this book is a story inspired by minimalism— discarding the superfluous. As I sorted through decades of photos, I came to see a clearer sense of my life. But this is not about my life so much as God's life in me, because the patterns and principles that make my life meaningful are available to anyone. This is the story of how God works in all of us when we allow him access.

But I'm getting ahead of myself.

The idea of sorting and, mostly, discarding a lifetime in photographs paralyzed me. Staring at the boxes, I saw nothing but chaos. But then Suzanne and I got an idea. Why not organize everything into piles based on where we lived? We had moved from California to Maine and back, with a significant tenure in the Upper Midwest.

With this approach I eliminated thousands of pictures— blurred, duplicates, or of people long forgotten. But I also identified hundreds of pictures of people and places that jogged memories of unimagined adventures and relationships, victories and defeats, joys and sorrows. The sorting process was emotionally draining at times, which surprised me. I would wake up at night dreaming of experiences from our past. Out of this troubling process, patterns emerged.

Looking back on my life at age seventy-two, I asked a fundamental question: What was the thread that connected the phases of my life? What was it that had directed me? The answer became clear. Each step was initiated by what Suzanne and I call a "Big Word." Big Words is my way of capturing the experience of God, clearly and without doubt, speaking to me, guiding my path, in ways that have been life changing, demanding, and always for the better. The Holy Spirit is the source of Big Words, filtered through diverse means: Scripture, preaching, prayer, dreams, visions, angels, those in authority, friends, casual comments, or God's small voice deep in the soul. They come with a promise of blessing, rooted in an intimate relationship with Christ.

Big Words usually came at life's crossroads—those moments of choice that defined my future. They came when I was seeking God, and they came when I was running from God. Sometimes their fulfillment was delayed for years which, despite doubt, deepened my faith. "Was that *really* God's voice? Yes, I know it was. What is he up to?"

Big Words were sometimes misunderstood or misinterpreted, only to be clearly understood after they were fulfilled. Some were risky and costly. They were never boring.

How do I know Big Words are God's voice? I just know. Jesus said, "My sheep hear my voice, and I know them, and they follow me" (John 10:27). I know Christ personally; he knows me intimately. He died for me; he was raised from the dead; and he is seated next to his Father, above all authority in heaven and on earth. He said, "Follow me, and I will guide you, lead you, speak to you, empower you. And you won't do it alone, you are a member of something bigger than yourself: the body of Christ, the church."

Big Words are the master keys to an adventure with God. Noah heard God's voice when told to build an ark. Abraham did not question God when directed to leave everything behind and move to the land God would show him. Moses obeyed God's Big Word at the burning bush to lead Israel out of Egyptian slavery. Mary trusted God's Big Word when an angel told her she would be the mother of Jesus. The Twelve Apostles heard Christ's call to "come and follow me" and they changed world history. Paul heard God's voice on the road to Damascus and was transformed from a persecutor to the persecuted. Every outstanding leader in the Bible received Big Words—life transforming words—from God.

Big Words are never big lies. Jesus promised, "I will ask the Father, and he will give you another Helper, to be with you forever, even the *Spirit of truth,* whom the world cannot receive, because it neither sees him nor knows him. You know him, for he dwells with you and will be in you" (John 14:16–17). The Holy Spirit, the Spirit of truth, confirms Big Words. And the Holy Spirit, working with the Word of truth—the Scriptures and confirming testimony of the church—forms a secure perimeter against falsehood and deception.

Every significant move of my life, each project or adventure, was initiated and fulfilled by God. My part was to listen to him and obey his call—not an easy task. I did not always follow through well, sometimes miscalculating and falling short, even losing courage at times. But his calls, his Big Words, were decisive, and his words trumped all other voices. I stuck with God and determined his voice and nothing else would shape my life. When I failed, he was there to lift me up.

Responding to Big Words means living an explorer's life. While sorting through pictures of my life, I carefully traced my geographic moves, first as a child carried along by my parents, later as an adult with Suzanne, tracking a journey that Jesus had MapQuested before my birth. All he required was my cooperation, my willingness to say, "Not my will but your will be done." That is easier said than done.

I'm inviting you to join Suzanne and me on our bumpy adventure, hoping that you discover one for yourself. There is no greater travel guide than Jesus because his destination is the City of God, the New Heavens and New Earth.

ONE

Set Apart

Milwaukee, Wisconsin
Birmingham, Michigan

"It's a good thing that God chose me before I was born,
because he certainly would not have afterwards."
—Charles Spurgeon, *The Spirit of Charles Spurgeon*

I was shaped in many ways by my parents. And so I will begin with my grandparents, who shaped my parents in so many important ways.

When Denna Miller walked into a room, her beauty—particularly her penetrating blue eyes—made people want to know her. She did not disappoint them; she was more than a Mona Lisa smile. With a confident personality and quick mind, Denna usually was the center of attention.

And when she met Karl Mathews, she knew what she wanted. Karl was a handsome, slight man, an inch shorter than Denna.

He also was reserved, rarely sharing his interior life. Opposites do attract.

Their relationship quickly bloomed into romance, and Denna got her man. They married on a Monday, June 5, 1911, at the First Methodist Episcopal Church in Danville, Illinois. Danville was a midpoint between Mattoon, Illinois (Denna's hometown) and Indianapolis, Indiana, where Karl was born, and where they had met.

After a short honeymoon, they settled down in Indianapolis, planning to have children immediately. More than anything, Denna wanted to be a mother.

Life rarely cooperates with our dreams. Years passed, World War I rocked the globe, and monthly disappointments turned to daily discouragement. Then, when she had lost almost all hope, in summer of 1916 Denna was blessed—actually, twice blessed. She was pregnant with twins.

On April 19, 1917, Denna and Karl became the parents of Elizabeth Ann and Mary Louise. But, like so much of Denna's life, joy was tarnished by grief: Mary Louise died shortly after birth. Tiny Elizabeth Ann survived, and immediately became the light of her mother's life—active, inquisitive, always competing with mom for center stage.

As the years passed Denna bonded deeply with her daughter. She and Karl tried in vain to have more children. But that was okay. They had Elizabeth Ann.

Then tragedy struck. One frigid morning in the fall of 1924, Denna, in her flowing nightgown, walked across the living room past seven-year-old Elizabeth Ann and close to an open-flame gas heater, common in those days. Denna's flammable nightgown touched the flames, and instantaneously she was engulfed in fire.

Her burning nightgown fused with her porcelain skin. The fire was over in a deadly flash. "I remember my dad putting mom in the bathtub filled with cold water," Elizabeth Ann said years later. "She died quickly and in agony."

Just like that, little Elizabeth Ann's life was changed forever.

Karl's life was changed too. He had carried a secret throughout their marriage. With Denna gone, Karl was through hiding. He was homosexual. Soon Andrew, who became known in the family as "Uncle Andy," moved in.

Uncle Andy was a kind man with a big smile, an extrovert like Denna. But for Elizabeth Ann, Uncle Andy could never replace her mother. This was 1925 Indiana, and for the next twelve years Elizabeth Ann struggled with confusion, anger, shame, and the fear of her family secrets being discovered by her classmates. And more than anything else, she missed her mother's love and care.

Witnessing the disastrous, violent death of her mother, the ongoing challenge of being raised by two gay men in 1920s and 30s Indiana, and the absence of a mother's compassion and unconditional acceptance resulted in emotional insecurity my mother carried for the rest of her life.

Under these circumstances, Elizabeth Ann turned to the only place she could find comfort and moral clarity: the Church. During her senior year at Shortridge High School, she completed her confirmation at the Advent Episcopal Church in May, 1936, and, after Bishop Joseph Francis laid hands on her, she received her first communion. Elizabeth Ann may have lost her earthly mother Denna, but now she was adopted by her heavenly Mother, the Episcopal Church.

A month after her confirmation, Elizabeth Ann graduated high school.

During her junior year at Shortridge High School, Elizabeth Ann had met William Noble Springer, Jr.—called Bill—a kind and engaging student. Everyone loved Bill.

Bill was the opposite of Elizabeth Ann's father Karl. She was immediately drawn to him and looked up to him. Literally. Elizabeth Ann was five-foot-two and beautiful; Bill was six-foot and handsome. Their attraction was mutual.

Descending from Hoosier stock, Bill was particularly proud of his "Noble" family heritage. He was a direct descendent of Noah Noble, the fifth governor of Indiana, and James Noble, the first US Senator from Indiana. Indiana's Noble County and the city of Noblesville were both named in honor of Bill's predecessors.

My paternal grandfather, also named William Noble Springer, lost his left arm when he was fifteen in a train accident—a loss from which he never fully recovered. Unresolved anger fueled depression and, later, abusive actions toward his family.

Six years later, Bill's father married Elizabeth Harris Archer in the Central Christian Church in Indianapolis. Elizabeth—called Momo by her grandchildren—had been raised in a wealthy family. Her relatives included a Congressional Medal of Honor winner (in the Civil War); successful businessmen; a President of the University of Indiana, University of Maine, and Butler University; physicians; the wife of a Prime Minister of England, and a poet (who, I presume, was not wealthy!).

Momo tended to be formal, dressed immaculately, and loved all things green. She was kind, but distant. She also held the family together and suffered through an unhappy marriage.

Shortly after marrying, Momo had a daughter, yet another Elizabeth—called Liba—Noble, and nine years later, on March 10, 1917, my father Bill was born. In her memoirs, Momo described my aunt

Liba and father Bill as "loving, devoted, smart, and religious . . . They were both baptized in the same pool in the Central Christian Church in which Noble and I were baptized before we met each other."

After high school in 1936, Bill took a job as a salesman. Because of the Great Depression, there was no money to attend college as his sister Liba had back in the 20s. But that did not deter or discourage Bill; his outgoing personality was made for sales. He was immediately successful. Two years later, on April 16, 1938, Bill and Elizabeth Ann married in the Anderson Methodist Church, just outside of Indianapolis.

Bill and Elizabeth Ann wasted no time starting a family. My mom gave birth to my sister Deena Kay (named for her grandmother, though spelled differently) in November 1939, then my brother Robert William (called Robin) in October 1943.

In 1946, my father's employer, E.C. Atkins and Company, transferred him to Milwaukee. He was doing well with the company, a real up-and-comer. This transfer was a promotion with more pay and responsibility. The Springers settled into the western suburb of Wauwatosa, and soon Elizabeth Ann was pregnant with their third child.

I was born on October 16, 1947 and named Kevin Noble. Kevin, for the sixth- to seventh-century Irish Saint Kevin of Glendalough. His name meant "of noble birth." I was also given the family name of Noble. Why I, and not my older

My mom, Elizabeth Ann, holding me
at my baptism, April 17, 1948

brother, was given the Noble name was never explained to me. Six months later I was baptized in Trinity Episcopal Church, the initiation of my long and fulfilling upbringing in the Episcopal Church.

Why This Family?

Most people at some point in their lives ask questions like, "Why was I born to *these* parents? At *this* time in history? In *this* culture?" I've certainly asked these questions, especially when I was struggling with my parents' unresolved dysfunctions and how they affected me. My father was a good man, but he had grown up without a healthy model of what it meant to be a husband and father. He wasn't prepared for the challenges of my mother's mercurial, narcissistic, controlling personality.

If you do not believe in God, the response to these questions is simple: I came into existence by the random union of two strands of DNA at conception. That is what makes me uniquely me. Nothing more, nothing less. Time and chance. You play the hand you were dealt. Fundamentally, you are on your own.

Of course, random selection frees us from the burden of seeking a transcendent meaning or purpose in life. Meaning and purpose are optional, though most people choose a purpose because, evolutionary psychologists hypothesize, a passion for purpose is built into our genes.

I am not suggesting that people who reject the idea of a transcendent God lack purpose. I believe this drive for more than mere survival—for significance—is something evolution cannot explain.

In any case, if you believe there is a God as I do, answers to the why questions become possible. God has something to say about this. He expressed his view to the prophet Jeremiah, over 2,500 years ago:

Before I formed you in the womb I knew you,
and before you were born I consecrated you;
I appointed you a prophet to the nations. **(Jeremiah 1:4–5)**

The Lord told Jeremiah he was not here by chance. God knew him before his conception—knew his parents, where and when he would be born, his gender, race, height, intelligence, personality—everything about him. And there is more: before Jeremiah was born, God consecrated him—set him apart—for something wonderful, for a specific purpose. Jeremiah was appointed "a prophet to the nations."

My calling has been different from Jeremiah's calling; it has been a unique calling fitted to me that gives me purpose. That is what this book is about: how I was called and shaped by Big Words. This story indicates how every man and woman in this world is set apart by God for a purpose that matters for eternity.

Some 450 years before Jeremiah, King David wrote the same truth in Psalm 139:13–16:

For you formed my inward parts;
You knitted me together in my mother's womb.
I praise you, for I am fearfully and wonderfully made.
Wonderful are your works;
my soul knows it very well.
My frame was not hidden from you,
when I was being made in secret,
intricately woven in the depths of the earth.
Your eyes saw my unformed substance;
in your book were written, every one of them,
the days that were formed for me,
when as yet there was none of them.

Listen carefully to these words "fearfully and wonderfully made" and "days that were formed for me." David says I was "made in secret, intricately woven"; by implication, he was designed carefully to fulfill his God-ordained purpose in his generation.

Both Jeremiah and David are saying that men and women have designer genes, donated to and nurtured in us by parents God chose before we were conceived.

That's good news and bad news.

My parents, particularly my father, were deeply committed to caring for me. But my mother's insecurities, high control, and erratic behavior were embarrassing and drove me inward. She was not easy to live with. When I was in high school, I had fantasies of a stranger calling me out of class to inform me that I was adopted and this amazing couple had come to reclaim me. If I were honest with myself, I thought I could have done a better job than God did in choosing my parents.

I never met my grandmother Denna, due to her horrific death, and I cannot remember my maternal grandfather, Karl, speaking a single word to me. I can barely remember meeting my paternal grandparents, William Noble and Elizabeth Harris Archer because (as I will explain) my father moved our family far away from them—deliberately putting distance between us and my grandfather because he was a dangerous man, most likely a child abuser—although I did not learn this until I was in my forties. This absence of grandparents was a tremendous deficit to me growing up.

So, why did God choose this family for me before "I was formed in the womb?" How can I make sense of it? Not that God owes me an explanation.

But here is how I see it now, with 20/20 hindsight. God used my mother's brokenness to drive her to the church, and she held on to that relationship for the rest of her life. She may have had only a mustard seed of faith, but God was the object of her trust—and God never let go of her. Her struggles alienated her from her children, but they never separated her from God's love. She insisted that I be baptized, attend church every week, and complete my confirmation.

Timothy Keller writes that what is essential in the process of becoming disciples of Jesus "is, to put it colloquially, becoming like the people we hang out with most." Because of my mother, the people I hung out with most were God fearing, men and women of integrity. They helped shape me into who and what I became.

My mother was also fiercely committed to her marriage. My parents were married imperfectly for fifty-two years, but only death separated them. My father cared for and loved my mom, who to the best of her ability loved my dad. Some psychologists say what kids want to know most is that they are loved by their parents. I believe it is just as important that children know their parents love each other. Confident, emotionally healthy children tend to come from devoted parents.

My mother wasn't always easy to love, but dad loved her nevertheless, sometimes to a fault. He decided that, come hell or high-water, he was committed to loving and protecting her.

I could write so much more but suffice it to say that I've come to peace with and have an appreciation for my parents. I don't have an exhaustive understanding of why I was born into my family, but this is an adequate understanding. And, perhaps most significantly, where they came up short, I have forgiven them.

On to Birmingham

In 1949, my father received another promotion and was transferred 375 miles east to Detroit. I was two years old. My family settled just north of Detroit in Birmingham (a fashionable city of 15,000), on Dorchester Road. Soon after, my mom gave birth to a third son, Scott Mathews.

Dorchester Road was loaded with young, professional families. Many of the men were business executives. This neighborhood was the first place I could venture out of the house, and the first person I met was Suzanne Nadal, another toddler who lived across the street. Like the Springers, Bob and Phyllis Nadal then had four children, two girls and two boys.

Suzanne's father, Bob, was part of the group of Harvard Business School graduates that Henry Ford II brought in after the Second World War to rebuild a company that had fallen on hard times. I loved being around Suzanne's family, especially her mother, Phyllis. She was kind and engaging, and she served the best snacks I had ever tasted. The Nadal's home was peaceful, happy, harmonious—where I wanted to be when not in my home.

Suzanne was six weeks older than I, and was baptized on March 28, 1948, by her paternal grandfather, William Thomas Nadal, known by the family as Poddy. He had earned his PhD at Harvard and eventually became president of Drury College (now Drury University) in Springfield, Missouri. When Poddy retired from Drury, he became a Congregational pastor. He and his wife Kathryn had hearts for God, something they passed on to Suzanne.

Suzanne and I were almost inseparable for three years. We played together and managed to get into our fair share of trouble. Those were the days when moms let their kids roam the neighborhood with no fear of danger.

One day Suzanne and I decided we could use some candy, so we hatched the idea that it would be easy to poach a few pieces out of the bins in a market three blocks away. (We were five years old.) I stood watch while Suzanne lifted the booty, and we got away with it.

We were walking home, smiling and enjoying the fruits of our sin, when my older brother Robin spotted us. He always suspected we were up to no good, and this time he was right. Stealing apples from a neighbor's tree is one thing, but grand theft from a grocery store crossed a line. He grabbed me by the ear (it hurts to this day), and ratted Suzanne out to her mom. We both had to confess to the store manager and pay for our sins.

Suzanne was my first friend, through thick and thin.

Birmingham is where I remember my first church, Christ Church Cranbrook, a beautiful, historic stone structure surrounded by lush gardens and lawns. The wooden pews, as is true of most Episcopal parishes, creaked when you sat down, stood, or kneeled through the liturgy. The colors were vibrant, the cross at the front of the church and liturgy thrilling. I had a sense of meeting God in every service, and the crucifix reminded me that Christ, the Son of God, died for me.

In 1952, my father became an employee of the Borg-Warner Corporation when it bought out Atkins & Company. Borg-Warner opened new opportunities for him, and he took advantage of them. He decided to take his young, growing family to a new, growing territory: southern California.

Once again, I was moving, and I had no control over the move. No more Suzanne. No more Christ Church Cranbrook. No more Birmingham or Dorchester Road. My dad decided we would drive the 2,300 miles across the country to experience the majestic mountains, deserts, and National Parks. Bob Nadal helped arrange a new Ford station wagon for the trip.

On the day we left, the entire neighborhood came out to send us off. Just before leaving, my mother called out Suzanne and said, "Suzanne, you have to kiss Kevin goodbye!" Reluctantly she stepped up as all the other children giggled. She kissed me on the cheek, we looked each other in the eye and sadly parted. My last memory of Birmingham was sitting in the far back of our station wagon, waving to Suzanne who was waving back. I thought, "I will never see her again."

Boy, was I wrong.

TWO

God, Baseball, Boy Scouts

Pacific Palisades, California

> *"To fall in love with God is the greatest romance;*
> *to seek him the greatest adventure;*
> *to find him, the greatest human achievement."*
> —Augustine of Hippo

Before moving west, my father carefully researched southern California communities, flying out and visiting the best places to raise a family. He chose Pacific Palisades, and he chose well.

Pacific Palisades, as its name implies, is nestled on steep bluffs overlooking the Pacific Ocean, with Malibu to the north, Brentwood to the east, Santa Monica to the south, and Catalina Island on the western horizon. Though part of the greater Los Angeles metropolitan area, because it has no direct freeway access, the Palisades, as locals call it, feels like a small town.

In 1952, there were only 15,000 people living in the Palisades' canyons and mountains, strung together along the scenic Sunset Boulevard, which connected Brentwood to the Pacific Coast Highway. The only other access to town was the steep Chautauqua Boulevard, snaking up from Will Rogers Beach. The weather is never too hot, never too cold, and almost always sunny except for seasonal morning fog, called May Gray and June Gloom. Having excellent schools, beautiful parks, epic beaches, and cafes—especially the Hot Dog Show and Dilly's Ice Cream—made Pacific Palisades a near-perfect environment for rearing kids.

Two parent families (divorce was rare in those days), sandlot baseball games, the the Fourth of July parade, surfing, and beach volleyball; that is the life that my father chose for us. Movie stars like Will Rogers, Spencer Tracy, Elizabeth Taylor, Ronald Reagan—and many more—have called the Palisades their home. University professors and Hollywood executives found it easy to maintain their anonymity in the Palisades and liked its proximity to Los Angeles. But my parents were neither famous nor wealthy compared to many of my friends' families.

On the surface, Pacific Palisades was probably what the creators of one of my favorite childhood television shows, *Leave It to Beaver,* had in mind. I identified with Theodore—the "Beaver"—who was always up to shenanigans but was somehow bailed out by his engaged and caring parents. Airing from 1957 through 1963, father Ward Cleaver's patient and sage advice solved weekly crises, while mom June cheerfully cleaned house and cooked three meals a day, wearing her hallmark pearls and waiting for Ward to "return home from the office." The Cleavers were the family I never had—indeed, nobody had—but a kid could dream, couldn't he?

During my senior year at Palisades High School, the January 29, 1965, issue of *Time* magazine ripped the Cleaver-family facade off the mythological perfection of Pacific Palisades. A cover article titled "On the Fringe of a Golden Era," illustrated by Andy Warhol, prominently featured quotes and observations from members of my graduating class. Hypothesizing Palisades High School might represent the country's best and brightest—if not most privileged—*Time* nevertheless found troubling questions lurking beneath the surface. The writers observed the usual problems of alcohol and drug abuse and sexual exploration but highlighted parental abdication:

> *"I don't get authority at home," sighs Dana Nye, seventeen, a student at Pacific Palisades High School in Los Angeles. "We're just a bunch of people who go about our business and live under one roof. One of these days I'd like to sit down and find out from my parents what they really believe in." What a lot of parents believe, as one mother expresses it, is that "a parent who says to a child 'I don't know' is somehow better than one who says, 'I know for sure.'"*

Jamie Kelso, a childhood friend of mine, was quoted as saying, "I'm kinda hoping to make a more meaningful person out of my mother, but it's hard work."

The unflattering picture was perhaps too harsh. Ten years later, my classmates Michael Medved and David Wallechinsky (author Irving Wallace's son) published the best-selling book *What Really Happened to the Class of '65?,* a follow-up on the students of Palisades High School. After that there was a television show of the same name, then another book in 1985, and countless articles in the *Los Angeles Times* and magazines. There were stories of successes and failures, a suicide of one of my closest childhood friends, and mental illness. The Palisades High School class of '65, my class, was the most analyzed, poked and prodded group of graduates in California if not the nation in the past seventy-five years.

I didn't need *Time* magazine to tell me most of my classmates had problems, but their shortcomings weren't my concern. I had my own problems: insecurities, fear of rejection and failure, pride, loneliness, shame, and guilt.

As I grew older, I became more conscious of these differences of wealth and social standing in the Palisades—and of where my family stood. By high school I struggled with feeling like an outsider, but I refused to let it defeat me. I also think that's why God gave me baseball, a sport that I excelled in throughout high school. Baseball gave me not only joy but also friends and the acceptance that every young man needs.

Starting organized baseball when only seven years old, I played for hours on the Palisades Park fields across the canyon from my home, learning teamwork and leadership. In those days kids played unsupervised sandlot baseball almost every morning of the summer. There were no adults to organize the teams and resolve conflicts. We had to do it ourselves, or we couldn't play. And no weaker player was ever left out; we needed the bodies to make complete teams.

So we would compete, argue, fight, laugh, and celebrate victories; and when the game was over, we'd reorganize and start again. These were some of the best days of my life. The heat of the afternoons was reserved for the beach—surfing and soothing our tired muscles.

But baseball also gave me something even more valuable, something I didn't recognize until looking at my Little League team pictures, which my mother saved. From Pee Wees through Minor League to Senior Little League, my dad coached every one of my teams. He is in every team photo. He didn't coach my higher division teams, but he attended almost every game. He supported, encouraged, commended, and corrected me. He taught me to never quit, be gracious in defeat and humble in victory. My father was my biggest fan. His care and love, which went beyond baseball, made it much easier to experience my heavenly Father's love as I grew up.

Mike Ferguson, Lynn Paddy, Mark Holmes, and me

More than Wealth and Good Weather

Shortly after moving to the Palisades, my parents joined St. Matthews Episcopal Church, which had just relocated from Swarthmore Avenue (the street I lived on) to the old Judy Garland estate, a bucolic forty-two-acre site a few blocks off Sunset Boulevard. Father Kenneth Cary was vicar and would remain my pastor until I graduated from Palisades High School.

In college I drifted away from the Episcopal Church, briefly becoming critical of my heritage. But in 1972, I had a conversation with Dr. Norman Grubb that changed my perspective of my religious upbringing. Dr. Grubb, an Englishman born in 1895, was, like me, raised in the Anglican Church—that is what the Episcopal Church is called in England and Canada. Dr. Grubb was a founder of Inter-Varsity (a ministry to college students) and World Evangelisation Crusade (W.E.C.); he also was an accomplished writer. (I thought he was ancient when we met for lunch, but he would live another twenty-two years and die at ninety-eight.)

During our conversation I made a derogatory remark about the Episcopal Church, and he interrupted me. "Allow me to ask you a question or two. Where did you learn that there is a God, and that God is Trinity?"

"St. Matthews."

"Where did you learn Jesus is God who became a man and died for your sins?"

"St. Matthews."

"Where did you learn Christ was raised from the dead and ascended to the Father? That the scriptures are the word of God? The Apostles' Creed? The Lord's Prayer? Where did you receive your first communion?"

St. Matthews, St. Matthews, St. Matthews.

Then he asked the clincher: "Do you believe God made a mistake putting you in the Episcopal Church? If not, I encourage you to thank God for what you received there and never speak against it again." To this day, I am grateful for my church upbringing, and specifically for my parents' church, St. Matthews.

Troop 223

St. Matthews Church was not the only formative influence in my life. Pacific Palisades was the home of Boy Scout Troop 223, led by its founder, Michael Lanning, an attorney by day who transformed into a boy discipling machine the rest of his waking hours. Mike made a promise to parents who were considering their sons joining Troop 223: "We promise we will make your boys better husbands and parents when they grow up, and CEOs, in the sense that they will receive qualified, formal leadership training and be given the chance to practice it. They will become community leaders." Mike's methods were remarkably simple and highly effective.

I was reminded of this when I attended an Eagle Court at the Riviera Country Club in the early 1990s. An Eagle Court is where Scouts receive their highest rank, Eagle, which is no small accomplishment, and few earn it. The Eagle candidates—seven at this evening's event—sat center stage with their individual sponsors surrounding them. Their sponsors were recent Eagles who mentored them through a multiyear journey, ascending the ranks of Scout, Tenderfoot, Second Class, First Class, Star, Life, and finally Eagle. The Scout Master, in this case Mike Lanning, oversaw the entire ceremony.

The general audience consisted of current Boy Scouts, parents, and friends. They were flanked by two smaller groups: First, those who had already earned their Eagles (I sat with that group of around ten men), and second, the Cub Scout Webelos, young, wide-eyed boys at the beginning of their Boy Scout adventure. To Mike

Lanning, the Webelos were akin to uncut diamonds, waiting to be formed into young men.

The Eagle Court was impressive. First, Mike Lanning welcomed everyone and then, looking squarely into the eyes of the perfectly still Webelos, said that someday if they chose to and were diligent, they would be Eagles. "This is what we will do to you. You can become like these boys." This was a vision casting, show-and-tell event. Mike also addressed my section, fellow Eagle witnesses, who were there to congratulate and welcome them into a club of honor for the rest of their lives.

Next, the mentors took over, one-by-one introducing each boy, describing highlights of their journeys with anecdotes that reflected on their character, humor, and personality. The candidate surmounted obstacles, failed at times, but never quit.

Finally, Mike oversaw each boy's formal reception of their Eagle. This was the most fascinating part of the ceremony for me. Each boy received a unique word; it felt like Mike prophesied over them. He said, "This is who this boy is—his unique strengths and gifts. He is prepared to be a leader, an influencer of others." Words matter, and Mike Lanning's words have influenced generations of boys who became better men in part because of his words.

Finally, their parents came forward, moms pinned the Eagle on them, they hugged, and the ceremony was over but never to be forgotten.

A Scout Is Reverent

When I was thirteen years old, I had an experience that changed my life. I had completed all the requirements for the penultimate rank of Life, except the interview. I was nervous going into the

BIG MOMENT JUST BEFORE THE PINNING of Eagle scout badges by mothers brings a quartet of young men of Troop 223, Pacific Palisades, to attention. All four received scouting's highest rank last Tuesday night in court ceremony at Methodist church Fellowship hall. Step by step from front are Mr. and Mrs. Alfred Tomkins of 708 Wildomar and son Michael; Mr. and Mrs. William Springer of 751 Swart avenue and son Kevin; Mr. and Mrs. Kenneth Thomps 535 Las Casas avenue and son Leif, and Dr. and Mrs Thee of 15301 DePauw street and son Jim. Scoutr Mike Lanning officiates—from the background. Cer brought to 54 number of Eagle Scouts in troop's six

My Eagle Court of Honor, September 26, 1961.
Mom and Dad are second up from the left, Michael Lanning is at the top

interview; three adult leaders were looking closely at my character. Toward the end of the interview, they asked me, "Of the Twelve Boy Scout Laws, which one is most important and why?"

I answered, "The first Scout Law: A Scout is Trustworthy. He tells the truth and keeps promises." I added a few words and they dismissed me, directing me to wait outside.

A few minutes later one of the interviewers came out and asked me a follow-up question: "We want you to reconsider your answer to the question about the most important Scout Law, reminding you that the last Law is 'A Scout is Reverent: Be reverent toward God. Be faithful in your religious duties.'"

I was mortified, but not because I could fail my Life rank. I had offended God. So, I apologized—to God and man. There is no higher rule of life than loving God. They told me had I not amended my answer, I would not have advanced to Life.

Hitchhiking Demerit Badge

Truth telling may not be the most important Scout Law, but it is nevertheless important. Around the time I was earning my Life rank, I violated that rule. It took me almost a lifetime to make it right.

In May 2015, while hiking along the Pacific Coast Highway, I recalled my youthful moral failure: I had cheated on my Hiking merit badge. Some fifty-three years earlier I hitchhiked twenty miles on the same highway and logged it as a required twenty-mile hike.

In my mind, I had *not* earned my Eagle. I was a cheat and a fraud.

So I sought out the current Scout Master of Troop 223, with the intention of returning my Eagle pin. I was astonished to discover that Mike Lanning, *my* Scout Master, was still leading Troop 223! Mike founded Troop 223 in 1954, and sixty-six years and over 840 Eagles later, he remained its leader. Mike Lanning is the Vin Scully of the Boy Scouts. In fact, it may be more accurate to say Vin Scully was the Mike Lanning of Major League Baseball play-by-play announcing!

I contacted Mike to inquire about meeting with him, and he graciously invited me to his Brentwood law office, not too far from where I now live—just a drive down the Pacific Coast Highway. As I drove to our meeting down the scene of my crime, I started sweating. I was nervous and ashamed. What would Mr. Lanning think? "I'm sixty-eight years old, but I feel like I'm thirteen again. It's irrational, but real!" Guilt and shame are powerful emotions. When I arrived at his office, he invited me to lunch at a little Italian restaurant across the street and encouraged me to call him Mike, not Mr. Lanning.

After catching up on our lives and finishing the meal, Mike looked at me and said, "Well, Kevin, why are you really here?" I took a deep breath, pulled out my precious Eagle pin, placed it on the table, and pushed it toward him. Then I spoke my carefully rehearsed speech: "Mike, I cheated on my Eagle, I didn't earn it, and I must return it to you today. I violated the first Scout Law. I was not trustworthy." With tear-filled eyes, I explained how perfect beach weather in Malibu was too much a temptation, so I hitch-hiked what was supposed to be a twenty-mile hike, surfed the day away, and lied about it.

Mike listened patiently—I was not the first Eagle to enter his confessional—and then asked a simple question. "How many merit badges did you earn?" The Eagle rank requires twenty-one merit badges, many of them specifically required and all difficult. "Twenty-six, Mike, I earned twenty-six."

"Well, Hiking is not a required merit badge for Eagle. So, you earned only twenty-five, but you completed the required twenty-one merit badges. You are still an Eagle."

Then he pushed my Eagle pin back across the table, and gently talked about honesty, soft hearts, and taking responsibility for mistakes. "Eagles aren't perfect, but they are humble. You are an Eagle."

Our meeting was over. And Mike Lanning insisted on paying the lunch bill.

Knowing About God

A solitary California Fan Palm sits in the front yard of 751 Swarthmore Avenue. It is the same tree, though much taller, that was there when I grew up. When the afternoon ocean breeze blows in, its tall, narrow trunk bows and sways like an orchestra conductor's baton against clear blue skies. As a child I would meditate on its beauty, poetic motion, remarkable strength, regularly sitting on the front lawn studying my palm tree and wondering, "How did it get here?" My beautiful tree symbolized creation, and I was starting to ask big questions, questions about the origin of creation, the order and beauty of my tree, the canyons, our beaches, and ocean. Mine were adolescent questions, but serious all the same. I was not questioning God's existence so much as probing my existence. What explains how the universe and I exist?

Knowing about God, Knowing God

On May 18, 1960, I was confirmed in St. Matthews Episcopal Church. A Suffragan Bishop from Pennsylvania laid hands on me, prayed over and blessed me, and Father Cary served me my first communion. Shortly after that I became an altar boy, serving with my older brother Robin for several years. I loved it. I loved God.

Big questions about God remained that my confirmation failed to answer. I thought, "God, I love you. Jesus is your Son, he died for our sins, he rose on the third day and is ascended to the Father. The Apostles' Creed says there is one God in three Persons, but that's difficult to comprehend." I could live with what I knew about God, and I could be patient about what I didn't know. I figured God was God, and I'm not.

But one question dogged me. I could not shake it, especially after praying the Lord's Prayer before bed every night, lying there thinking I knew *about* God, but I didn't know him *personally*, like a friend. I felt he was close to me, but I was far from him. Something was missing. God was more an idea than an experiential reality. I wanted more.

I had a hunger for "something more"—some call it a hunger for God—a need in my soul to experience God himself. Wanting the far-away God that I believed in to come close to me, my heart had a spiritual vacuum, and I did not know how to fill it. I desired to know God so intimately that I could hear his voice, respond to his calling, feel the weight of his character, and have great, daring adventures with him and for him.

Billy Graham

Then something happened to my mother that would change my life. In September 1963, a friend invited her to attend a Billy Graham Crusade at the Los Angeles Memorial Coliseum. The next day she announced to the family that she had entered a "personal relationship with Jesus." She also said a church bus was going to take another group of folks to the Coliseum on Sunday evening. She insisted I attend. "Well," I thought, "perhaps this is an answer to my quest of knowing God personally and hearing his voice."

I didn't want to go alone. That problem was solved when the first baseman on my high school baseball team said he was going. And that's how I ended up in the largest crowd ever to attend an event at the Los Angeles Memorial Coliseum, on September 8, 1963: 134,254 people, with another 20,000 outside listening on loudspeakers in Exposition Park. It was the largest crowd I would ever experience. But when Dr. Graham started speaking from Daniel 5, about the story of Belshazzar and the writing on the wall, it was like he was speaking only to me.

That night when Dr. Graham explained the writing on the wall in Daniel 5, God's message to Belshazzar: "Mene, Mene, Tekel,

Upharsin"—you have been numbered, weighed and your life is divid-ed—I knew in my heart that word described me. I came up short of God's standard. The burden of guilt from sin, failure, and shortcom-ing was amplified by the beauty and righteousness of God. That is why Jesus died on the Cross—to bridge the gap between me and his Father! I had looked at the cross every week at church, but only now understood what it meant to me personally. I felt like he was saying, "You are unique! *You are blessed.*" This was an aha moment.

The gospel message made perfect sense, though it was coun-terintuitive. It was bad news/good news. Bad news: I'm a sinner. Good news: acknowledging I'm a sinner opens the door to friend-ship with God—the gap between me and God's glory was closed that day. I had sought him in heaven, and Jesus met me in the Col-iseum. The moment I believed, scales fell from my eyes. I could talk to him, and he talked to me. That night I thought I got God; actually, God took hold of me. Jesus brought heaven to earth.

Conversion is remarkable. One minute I was alienated from God; the next I was his friend. My relationship with God was trans-formed from a concept to a reality. I didn't merely believe in God; I believed God. And this was because of what God did for me at the Cross, not because of what I did for God.

I heard his voice, responded, and confessed, "Jesus, my life is now given to you, completely. You gave your life for me, so I give my life to you. Do with me as you wish." The weight of his glory overwhelmed me with peace and joy; I was changed forever. In a flash, the world looked different and would never again look the same. In that moment, I entered the fulness of life in the presence of God. I was a most eager convert.

I had never tried to earn a relationship with God—that was, for me, an impossible task. I had been taught, and believed, Christ died for my sins. But I had struggled with the chasm between God and me, and with the fear of not knowing what would happen to me when I die. That night I realized that Christ's death and resurrection changed *everything*. I no longer needed to fear eternity.

That is a Big Word. Christ called me to himself. "Now," in the words of Malcolm Muggeridge, "was becoming always," which took the heat off an unsure future and certain death and separation of God. By allowing Jesus to invade my heart, I could be present in every moment of every day in every relationship, because my future was secure.

My life became an unimagined adventure that day.

September 8, 1963, the Los Angeles Memorial Coliseum, where I responded to the gospel when Billy Graham spoke from the Old Testament prophetic book of Daniel

"What about You?"

There were so many people jammed into the Coliseum, I could not "walk forward," as was customary at Billy Graham Crusades for those who wanted to respond to God. In response to Dr. Graham's call, I stood up, prayed, and then looked to my left at my friend who remained seated, and I exclaimed, "This is it! This is what I've been looking for! Christ makes life worth living. Knowing God, forgiveness, hearing his voice, walking with him, eternal life. *What about you?*" Within ten seconds after committing my life to Christ, I witnessed to my friend. I wanted him to know the joy of knowing God. My first words after meeting the Word, Jesus, were to testify to God's love for humanity.

He mumbled something about not responding because he didn't want to be put on a mailing list. He couldn't hear. He couldn't see. Our relationship was never the same after that, though not by my choice.

I learned immediately that obeying a Big Word wasn't going to win me many popularity contests. The good news of Christ can be as much a divider as a unifier. But for me, the die was cast; nothing could change what had started the night of September 8, 1963. I was caught by Christ, and there was no escaping, and no desire on my part to escape.

THREE

Shattered Dreams

Los Angeles, California

"If we answer the call to discipleship, where will it lead us? What decisions and partings will it demand? To answer this question we shall have to go to him, for only he knows the answer. Only Jesus Christ, who bids us follow him, knows the journey's end. But we do know that it will be a road of boundless mercy. Discipleship means joy."
—Dietrich Bonhoeffer, *The Cost of Discipleship*

I n the seventh grade, I knew what I wanted to do with my life. After graduating from high school, I was going to enroll at the University of California at Los Angeles (UCLA), major in biology, then attend medical school. Our family doctor, Lloyd Thee, took me under his wing and mentored me. He was my hero, my model.

After committing to Christ at the Billy Graham Crusade at age fifteen, the thought never entered my mind to submit my life dream to him. I assumed he'd bless my noble intentions. But when I said, "I surrender to you," God took me at my word and took hold of my life.

Palisades High School was academically competitive, but I survived and was admitted to UCLA. It looked like I was off to a good start. Unfortunately, I failed to understand that giving everything to God meant his taking control in real time. His agenda, I soon learned, was not my agenda. Clearly I had not understood the implications of surrendering my life to God.

That is when I discovered that God can be a dream wrecker.

This started with my parents refusing to sign off on my attending UCLA. I had skipped a grade in elementary school, so I was only seventeen years old as a college freshman and needed their signature to enroll. I was crushed.

Then they announced they were selling our home in Pacific Palisades and moving to the San Fernando Valley, and they wanted me to enroll at nearby Pierce Community College. Junior college? Living at home? Now I was in free fall.

I prayed, "God, what are you doing? I needed help with my plans, and you did this to me?"

God's response: crickets.

Shattered dreams are frequently followed by bitterness and resentment. I had both in spades, mostly toward my parents. Nevertheless, I enrolled at Pierce College (it was that or get drafted and sent to Vietnam), deciding to apply myself and then transfer in a year to UCLA.

The first year went well academically, but bad spiritually. I was isolated, without friends and wracked with self-pity. Somehow, I got through my freshman year, and then my parents again said they would not financially support me to attend UCLA. They thought I still wasn't ready to leave home.

Life is a series of choices. Most are inconsequential, part of the humdrum of daily living: Should I eat Italian or Mexican tonight? Should I drive to work on the slower, scenic route or the faster, boring freeway? But a few choices are crossroads. Should I marry that woman? Should I change my career? These choices result in profound and lasting change. These are forks in the road—monumental moments in life—like Julius Caesar's crossing the Rubicon river in 49 BC and starting a civil war. "Every once in a while," Oswald Chambers observed, "God brings us to a... great crossroads in our life. From that point we either go toward a more and more slow, lazy, and useless Christian life, or we become more and more on fire, giving our utmost for his highest—our best for his glory."

I faced one of those moments at the beginning of my sophomore year in college. Around this time mom and dad went away for the weekend, and I decided I had had enough. I wanted to leave home and school, thinking I'd be better off without my parents. Not consulting God and assuming he understood, I packed my car (which they owned) and drove down the hill.

A mile or two away, just before entering the Ventura Freeway, I sensed that God wanted to speak a Big Word. At last! Pulling the car over, I listened. "If you enter the freeway and leave home, your life will never be the same. You will change the direction of your life. And it will not be for the better." This was my crossing the Rubicon moment.

God's voice broke me. He did not demand that I turn around, he simply told me that the long-term consequences of my rebellion would not be good. This Big Word was a warning. I had a choice. His plans or my dreams. Sitting by the side of the road and weeping from disappointment, I turned around and returned home. The pain was incalculable. In the words of Lucy Shaw, "Faith meant giving up my closely held control of my life and destiny." God was calling me into uncharted waters—my desires or his will? My road or his? That choice was a part of knowing God I had not yet learned. It took a Big Word to drive the painful truth home. I took the U-turn back into his will.

Bloom Where You Are Planted

I decided to make the most of where God had placed me. The pain was not going to paralyze me. Still keeping my full academic schedule, I chose to fight isolation by trying out for the baseball team. I had hit .365 in high school and was a solid defensive player. I thought I was good enough to make the team.

College baseball is on a much higher level than high school, and players have a different attitude. Pierce College has an outstanding baseball tradition, producing Major League players like Rick Auerbach, Doug DeCinces, Barry Zito, and Coco Crisp after I played there. Most of my teammates were grown men hoping to become professional baseball players, leaving little time for friendships.

Having taken a year off from baseball, I felt uneasy when coach Joe Kelly started hitting balls to me at second base. After a few minutes, he directed me to move to my right, over to shortstop. I had grown two inches since graduating high school, and six feet was a nice size for a middle infielder. With my range and strength, I had no problem making the required throws and—much to my surprise—was named the starting shortstop. All those hours of sandlot baseball at Palisades Park paid off.

With a fifty-eight-game schedule, baseball kept me busy. There was no time left to feel sorry for myself, which was a good thing. As the season wore on, I wore down, mentally and physically. My temperament was not suited for the pros; I needed more intellectual stimulation. By the end of the season, I was burnt out. But I was glad to get baseball out of my system. In the words of Paul, "When I became a man, I gave up childish ways" (1 Corinthians 13:11).

My academics were strong enough to get into UCLA for my junior year. However, my college advisor thought it would be a good idea to apply to other colleges. The only one that interested me was the University of Southern California (USC), but it was a costly private school. I had never considered USC because it was unaffordable. "They have academic scholarships. You have the grades and background to earn one." So I applied to UCLA and USC.

A few weeks later I received a big envelope in the mail, informing me I had been awarded a full academic scholarship to USC. Immediately this UCLA Bruin became a USC Trojan. I was beginning to realize that God did have a plan for my life.

Come, Holy Spirit

The summer before matriculating at USC I was invited to attend a week-long retreat at Arrowhead Springs in the mountains above San Bernardino, sponsored by Campus Crusade for Christ (now called Cru). The theme of the week was evangelism, with training how to be witnesses for Christ that culminated in going to Newport Beach and sharing the gospel with young people.

The night before we were driven to the beach, Bill Bright, Crusade's founder and president, presented a teaching session about the Holy Spirit. His points were simple: we cannot successfully live the Christian life in our own strength; the Father has sent the Holy Spirit to empower us; we are commanded in Ephesians 5:18 to "be filled with the Holy Spirit."

Three-hundred students from all over the country filled the room, but I felt like an audience of one. I suffered from a power outage in my life, lacking the strength to live fully for Christ. That night I could hardly sleep, intermittently waking and thinking about Dr. Bright's Big Word. By one o'clock I was wide-eyed. God was calling me to open my heart fully to the Holy Spirit. So, I slipped out of bed, dressed, and found a quiet place under a lonely palm tree—where else?—on the hotel grounds, near an illuminated swimming pool.

Unsure of what to expect, my hunger for God motivated me to pray. "Holy Spirit," I pleaded, "I have been living in my own strength too long. Now I yield every part of my life to you. Come and fill me."

What happened next was beyond anything I had been taught about how God works. First, I felt a rush of power come over my body, a warm tingling feeling I had never experienced. With that rush came a peace and an urge to worship God. As I began worshipping, I was soon speaking in tongues, though for the first few minutes I was unsure of what it was. Tongues is a Holy Spirit inspired form of prayer in an unknown language to the person praying but is understood by God. The apostle Paul prayed in tongues, writing in First Corinthians 14:14, "If I pray in a tongue, my spirit prays but my mind is unfruitful." After praying and worshipping for an hour, I opened my Bible and began reading . . . and reading . . . and reading into the early morning. Scripture came alive; the word of God leapt off the pages.

The next morning, I told no one of my experience. "Was it real?" It had to be. I had an unusual confidence in God, unlike anything I had ever experienced before. Somewhat confused about the meaning of what had happened the night before, I decided I'd sort it out later. As the time to go to the beaches approached, the gospel burned in my heart, pressing every part of my being with an urgency to witness about Jesus Christ.

I boarded the bus a bit apprehensive about talking with strangers. At least we were sent out in pairs. When my partner Bob and I hit the beach, we approached two Hispanic teenage boys, asking if they would participate in a religious survey. The survey was part of the evangelism program, a way of beginning conversations with strangers. Soon they were talking about Jesus Christ. Two girls joined the conversation, then another three boys. I received words from God—I can only describe it that way—about the teenagers' sins and God's grace.

As I spoke, my insights about the teenagers were right on target. In the Bible these insights are called words of knowledge, although I didn't know that at the time. Supernaturally knowing what their greatest needs were, I spoke with authority about God's love and righteousness in a way that opened their hearts. I was careful not to shame any of them, only to say enough for them to realize their need for God's grace. Bob stood by, astonished.

Within half an hour several of the teenagers were weeping, falling to their knees, repenting of their sins, and turning to Christ. Before the day was over at least a dozen young people made Christian commitments. In several instances students who initially joined the conversation only to mock and ridicule me ended up on their knees and repenting.

Afterwards, Bob asked me, "What happened to you?"

Big Words that are obeyed benefit the world in which we live. But the world does not always receive God's offer of eternal life. I learned this lesson the day I returned home from Arrowhead Springs and met with a close college friend. He patiently listened as I shared the gospel with him, as I had done on the beach. "Are you finished?" he asked me. "Yes," I responded. And then he said, "I will never talk to you again." And he did not. I was dead to him.

His response was a sobering reminder that unless God gives us "eyes to see and ears to hear" the truth of the kingdom of God, we will not receive the good news that Christ died on the cross for our sins. I felt the sting of rejection, but then I realized my friend rejected not me but Christ. I was only an errand boy delivering the message.

USC

Shortly after my Newport Beach experience, I enrolled in USC. To avoid the isolation trap that I had fallen into at Pierce College, I sought friendship in the Campus Crusade student group. Christianity, I concluded from Scripture, was meant to be experienced in community. I heeded the warning of Proverbs 18:1, "Whoever isolates himself seeks his own desire; he breaks out against all sound judgment."

At Crusade I met staffer Ray Nethery, who was in his late thirties. He would become my mentor, pastor, close friend, and he remains so to this day. Ray is in his nineties as I write this and going strong. We live two thousand miles apart but talk regularly.

The USC Crusade chapter was small, and I quickly became the primary leader. Ray suggested we work more closely with the larger UCLA chapter to reach our campuses more effectively for Christ. That is where I met UCLA students Steve Patterson and Clyde Kilgore. The three of us caught a vision for community, convincing Hav Larson—a wealthy businessman from Pacific Palisades—to purchase an old fraternity house in Westwood and convert it into a student gathering place. The fraternity was rebranded the "JC

Light and Power House," and this was where I got my first taste of in-depth Christian relationships. Junior year was exhilarating—study, fellowship, and campus outreach filled every moment of my life. Senior year would get even better.

The Girl from Rolling Hills

As the small, second-floor lecture hall in the Bovard Building filled up for the first meeting of the required senior-year European history class, I was stretched out in a chair next to the window, focused on the football team practice on the field below, specifically their running back O.J. Simpson. If I had turned around and noticed the girl who walked in and sat a row or two behind me, I wouldn't have recognized her.

The class was composed of a small number of disparate majors, and the professor did something unusual. He asked each of the twenty-five or so students to introduce themselves, telling where they went to high school and their majors. I was one of the first to speak. "Kevin Springer. Palisades High School. Biology."

I immediately noticed when the girl behind me shot up in her seat. She wouldn't take her eyes off me. "That's strange," I thought. "Hey, she's cute. She looks like a blond Twiggy." (Twiggy was a willowy super-model of the moment from England.)

When it was her turn, she said, "I'm Suzanne Nadal. I went to Palos Verdes High School, and I'm a French major." And, looking squarely at me, she blurted out, "Are you the Kevin Springer from Dorchester Road in Birmingham, Michigan, that I grew up with?"

My response was swift, "If you kissed me on my cheek before my family moved to California, I'm that Kevin Springer." I never forgot her kiss; it was my first and if truth be told, one of my only kisses. The other students were entertained.

God had gone to a lot of trouble to get Suzanne and me together. My dream school was UCLA, but he shattered that dream to place me at USC. Suzanne's dream school was Stanford. She was not admitted out of high school but had gained admittance as a transfer student. She should have been at Stanford that fall, after studying abroad at the University of Strasbourg in France the previous year. But when Stanford required that she wait until winter term to enroll, she returned to USC. So here we were, sitting in this odd class outside our majors.

After class we found a quiet bench and talked and talked. And something remarkable happened. We became instant friends, like we were six-years old again. Over the next few weeks we greatly enjoyed hanging out, talking about what was profoundly important in our lives. We rediscovered a friendship, not merely of distant memories but shared values. C. S. Lewis wrote, "Friendship is born at that moment when one person says to another, 'What? You too? I thought I was the only one.'" We let each other in on what we were thinking, without fear of rejection.

I shared about my relationship with Christ, and specifically my 1963 conversion experience at the Billy Graham crusade at the nearby Los Angeles Coliseum. Suzanne responded, "I was at that same crusade, only on a different night. And I too heard God's voice and committed my life to Christ."

"What? You too?"

A few weeks into the fall, Suzanne joined our USC Christian group, no longer affiliated with Crusade as key staff had resigned to pursue other ministries. I noticed that she was consistently putting Christ first in her life. Though still living near USC, we got involved in the fellowship and teaching at the JC Light and Power House in Westwood, and strategized about reaching our campus for Christ.

Around this time, we heard Jon Braun, formerly the national field coordinator for Crusade, speak on "Sex, Love, and Marriage." He was the most dynamic and effective speaker we had ever heard. He spoke for three nights at the University of California at Santa Barbara campus, drawing 300 students the first evening, and 3,000 the last evening—with many conversions. We thought, "Why not bring Jon to USC?" After praying, we concluded fraternity row would be a strategic location, and Suzanne's old sorority, the Tri-Deltas, was the ideal venue. The Tri-Delta house was centrally located and large. They agreed to host Jon Braun for an evening.

We promoted the event at the Greek houses and on campus. I personally invited members of the Students for a Democratic Society (SDS), a radical leftist students' group, to attend. When the night came, the Tri-Delta house was packed with men and women. Four or five SDS students sat in the front row.

Jon opened his message with these words, "When it comes to sex, you are either in or out." A roar of laughter hit the room, and everyone came to rapt attention. For the next hour Jon took the raucous crowd on a roller coaster ride that ended with the gospel. That was one of the craziest nights I have ever experienced. When Jon spoke, I heard God's voice that was relevant to my generation. I sensed that is what God was calling me to do with my life—speak the gospel boldly and relevantly to my generation.

That fall, Suzanne and I were not boyfriend and girlfriend. I was casually seeing a UCLA student I met through Crusade, while Suzanne was dating a couple of old flames. Neither of us was serious about the people we were seeing.

We occasionally spent weekends at her parents' home in Rolling Hills and met alone regularly for picnic lunches in the Exposition Park Rose Garden next to campus. We were true friends, nothing more, not that others did not suspect something more might be brewing. One Rolling Hills weekend while I was spending time with her younger brother Jim, Suzanne's father asked her, "What's going on with Kevin? It looks like more than friendship is happening there." Suzanne denied it, as I would have if he had asked me. We were clueless.

Rose Garden Revelation

Then one day during one of our Rose Garden picnics, we talked about what we were looking for in a wife or husband. I suggested we compose a list of attributes. My list described her; her list described me. We were speechless. But should we have been? Perhaps not. If we had enjoyed each other's company from ages three to six, why wouldn't we be attracted to each other fifteen years later?

We were quite similar in some traits. For example, we both are orderly and hardworking, and we are extroverts, though I more than Suzanne. And we are open to new ideas and new people. We genuinely enjoy meeting and hosting all types of people, almost always discovering something positive and interesting in them.

On the other hand, we complement each other. Suzanne is emotionally steady while I am prone to mood swings. She keeps me from going off the rails when facing difficult challenges. Bottom-line: we liked each other and made a good team when we were six, and when we were twenty-one. We were a perfect fit.

In addition to her heart for God, I loved that Suzanne was my equal. She was no shrinking violet. When God created Eve in the Garden of Eden, he didn't take a bone from Adam's head so she would dominate him; nor did God create her from a bone in his foot, so he would dominate her. God created Eve from Adam's rib, close to his heart, a place of intimacy and equal standing. Eve was a perfect fit for Adam, and when he saw her, he said, "This is at last a bone of my bones and flesh of my flesh." That's what I prayed for in a wife. And God gave Suzanne to me.

Friendship had opened the door to a deeper relationship with God, then intimacy with one another, and finally deep, romantic feelings. We were called to advance God's kingdom, perfect complements, and we were head over heels in love.

We made plans to get married as soon as possible.

Suzanne's parents were skeptical about how quickly we wanted to marry. I don't blame them. One day Suzanne is thinking of going back to Yale to visit a former high school date, the next she announces she wants to marry Kevin. One day, Kevin is seeing a UCLA girl, the next . . .

Our senior year at USC, looking forward to a bright future

Father of the Bride

I wanted to ask Suzanne's parents for permission to marry her; we wanted, we *needed*, their blessing. So, we arranged a luncheon at Suzanne's home. We were nervous; I could barely finish my bowl of chili. Tension in the room was palpable.

Alberta Keeby, who had worked for and lived with the Nadal family since their Michigan days, served the meal and retreated to the kitchen. Suzanne had confided everything to Alberta; she always had an encouraging word and prayer. After a minute or two, the swinging kitchen door cracked open an inch. Suzanne's mother quietly said, "Alberta." The door just as slowly squeaked closed, though not all the way. We could feel her prayers.

As all four of our spoons descended in unison, Suzanne's father Bob looked at me and said, "Well, Kevin." This could have been a scene in the movie *Father of the Bride*. Taking a deep breath and glancing toward Suzanne, I popped the big question. Suzanne's dad, a tall, dignified man, listened intently and asked a few questions about money (we had none). He said, "Do you think twenties will float down out of heaven?" Then her mother, Phyllis, jumped in and saved the day. "Yes! Of course, you may marry our daughter." They blessed our marriage!

Parental blessing imparts God's favor and protection; it is something that brings well-being to a new marriage. We wanted it; we needed it from both sets of parents. My father told me, "If you don't marry Suzanne, it will be the biggest mistake of your life." In our ceremony on March 29, 1969, Suzanne's father Bob, in response to Pastor Jon Braun's question, "Who gives this woman to be married to this man," said, "Her mother and I do." He then put her hand in mine, and a spiritual reality was announced to the world, seen and unseen, that we were leaving our parents and starting a new family.

That day a new team was inaugurated to advance God's kingdom. For more than fifty years we have experienced Solomon's wisdom that "two are better than one":

Two are better than one, because they have a good reward for their toil. For if they fall, one will lift up his fellow. But woe to him who is alone when he falls and has not another to lift him up! Again, if two lie together, they keep warm, but how can one keep warm alone? And though a man might prevail against one who is alone, two will withstand him—a threefold cord is not quickly broken **(Ecclesiastes 4:9–12)**.

We honeymooned for five days in Blue Jay, near Arrowhead Lake in the San Bernardino Mountains. When I paid the $90 for our cabin, my check bounced. Suzanne, the daughter of a Harvard MBA, was mortified. After that she took oversight of our finances, never relinquishing the role. We have never had another check bounce.

One of our first marriage acts was to get on our knees and submit to God. "God," we prayed, "you are first in our lives. We don't expect each other to be perfect, and where we fall short, we will forgive each other." Our relationship has been a threefold cord ever since.

Our marriage day, March 29, 1969, Rolling Hills, California

FOUR

It's a Small Town

Eastport, Maine

"I have one desire now—to live a life of reckless abandon
for the Lord, putting all my energy and strength into it."
—Elisabeth Elliot, *Through Gates of Splendor*

After marrying, Suzanne and I continued at USC to finish our degrees. We paid $80 per month for a one-bedroom apartment near campus and lived there for two glorious months.

We faced uncertain times. The Vietnam war and social unrest gripped the country. My student deferment would be up in June, which made me a prime candidate for the draft. Sensing God might be calling me to ministry, I put medical school on hold. My senior advisor, Dr. Walter Martin, encouraged me to pursue a PhD in Marine Biology. Suzanne's French professor encouraged her to get a PhD. So many options. No answers. But we had confidence God was in control.

Suzanne and I needed a Big Word, and we received one when reading from Deuteronomy 24:5. While this Scripture was specifically written for Israel, the Holy Spirit said it applied to *our* marriage in that unique time. The wisdom of this verse hit us like a lightning bolt!

> When a man takes a bride, he must not go out with the army or be liable for any duty. He is free to stay at home for one year, so that he can bring joy to the wife he has married. (HCSB)

Newly married? Check. Do not join the army? Check. Focus for one year on making my wife happy? Check! That was a Big Word, the direction for the first year of our life together.

The Lord said take a year to build a foundation that will last a lifetime. Following Christ's words, we committed to leaving and cleaving—leaving our parents and holding fast to each other (Matthew 19:5). We were freed from the burden of graduate school or the army. Those decisions would come later.

Suzanne and I prayed and planned. "Lord," we prayed, "we love you. You have shown us your will from Deuteronomy 24:5. Now show us your way. Send us where you want us. Our lives are yours." We thought it would be exciting to go to another part of the country and teach for one year in a poor area, preferably a small town. But where to go?

Around this time a fellow USC student from Philadelphia shared that his family spent every summer on the Down East coast of Maine. He thought there might be a town in need of teachers. He mentioned three cities: Bar Harbor, Machias, and Eastport. We looked them up on a map and wrote each school district offering our services.

Much to our surprise, Eastport immediately responded. They needed a French and English teacher, and a biology and physical science teacher. This was a perfect fit. Our annual salary was $5,500 each.

Eastport was a hardscrabble fishing town of 2,000 souls in Washington county, the poorest county in New England. The city sat on an island overlooking the Bay of Fundy. The eastern-most city in the United States, Eastport is the farthest point from Los Angeles in the contiguous states. After negotiating a travel allowance of $200, we signed contracts. God was sending us on our first assignment. This was the adventure we were looking for!

3,500 Miles and Back to the Past

In July 1969, we packed Suzanne's deep-red Ford Cortina—named Kirschen (cherry in German)—said tearful goodbyes to family and friends, and started to drive north before going east. We wanted to see the country, visit relatives and friends, and camp along the way.

After sightseeing in San Francisco, we visited Suzanne's cousins, Dick and Barbara, in Trinidad Bay and hiked the verdant Fern Canyon. From there we headed to Bozeman, Montana and friends; the Black Hills in South Dakota; and Green Bay, Wisconsin. Then we caught a ferry across Lake Michigan and on to Frankfort, Michigan. Growing up in Michigan, Suzanne had spent fourteen summers in Frankfort at her grandparents' summer cottage, called Katomco, on Lake Michigan. This was an emotional experience for her, full of many joyous memories.

Continuing east, we visited our old neighborhood on Dorchester Road in Birmingham, walking the streets holding hands as we had as little children. We then crossed over the border into Ontario, Canada, where we found a beautiful provincial campground. The night was crystal-clear in Ontario on July 20, when Neil Armstrong piloted the lunar module *Eagle* onto the Sea of Tranquility and, at 10:56 p.m., stepped out on the moon. A neighborly camper jerry-rigged his portable, black-and-white television with rabbit ears; we crowded around, watching as Neil said those famous words, "That's one small step for man, one giant leap for mankind." Directly overhead was the fullest moon I have seen to this day. Our adventure felt like a giant road trip for Jesus.

The next day we were on to Niagara Falls—after all, we were newlyweds—and then down to Mansfield, Ohio, to visit Ray and Eunice Nethery. The Netherys had recently moved from California to Mansfield to start an outreach ministry to college students modeled off Francis and Edith Schaeffer's L'Abri community in Switzerland. Suzanne and I were attracted to the new ministry because we had developed a heart for outreach, discipleship, and community at the JC Light and Power House in college. In Mansfield we met many like-minded young couples and singles.

After a week in Mansfield, we needed to keep moving. Eastport's Shead Memorial High School was opening soon, and we had a thousand miles ahead of us. Before leaving Ohio, we visited my Uncle Charlie in Cleveland, which was a powder keg of racial tension. When we made a wrong turn from the freeway, a policeman escorted us to Uncle Charlie's home. The weather was hot and sticky, tensions high, and people angry. The frustrated and frightened police officer said, "What are you trying to do, start a riot?"

After a couple of days with Uncle Charlie, we were off through Erie into upstate New York, crossing the Green Mountains of Vermont and New Hampshire. Upper New England was more beautiful than we had imagined.

Finally, we entered Maine, taking Route 9, affectionally known as the Airline Road, undulating ninety miles straight through dense forests from Bangor to Calais—cutting deep into the heart of Washington county. Arriving in what we thought was Calais, we pulled into a gas station and asked the attendant, "Is this Cal-ay," using the French pronunciation of Calais.

Scratching his head, he gave us a puzzled look. "Nope, never heard of Cal-ay."

"Well, what's the name of this town?"

"Cal-is."

Welcome to Down East Maine.

After gassing Kirschen we drove twenty-seven miles along the St. Croix River, through the tiny town of Perry, then Pleasant Point—reservation home of the Passamaquoddy Tribe, population 300. To enter Eastport, we used a causeway that passed Half Moon Cove. Half Moon Cove was known for its expansive mud flats—perfect for digging clams—uncovered daily by some of the most powerful tidal forces in the world.

Now on the outskirts of Eastport, a city of twelve-square miles (only 3.63 square miles of which is land) consisting entirely of islands and rugged coastline, dangling in the frigid waters of the Bay of Fundy, our first impression of Eastport was—to be charitable—a town in decline. The population had diminished more than 20 percent in the previous ten years, mostly due to the failing fishing industry. In the not-too-distant past, Eastport had been an Atlantic Seaboard center of sardine canning, supporting thirteen factories. When we arrived, only one remained operational; the others were decaying carcasses of a prosperous past. There was lobster fishing and some port activity—Eastport is home to the deepest natural harbor in the lower forty-eight—but jobs were few and far between, and mostly seasonal.

Aging and rundown, Eastport was not a picture-postcard New England town, but it would now be our home. We could not have chosen a place more different from southern California in climate, culture, economics, and education.

It's a Small Town

Before we had left the West Coast, the school board was kind enough to connect us with Ed and Lillian Bartlett, who owned one of Eastport's few rental properties. We thought it was strange that they were standing on their front lawn as though they were expecting us when we drove up to their home on Clark Street—until we

Crossing Half Moon Cove into Eastport, Maine, August 1969

learned they *were* expecting us. From the time we crossed town limits, everyone knew via the party phone lines (a half dozen families shared one line) that the Californians had arrived—Kirschen's California plates and downhill skis gave us away.

This was our introduction to small town life.

Ed and Lillian, who were in their early fifties, were generous landlords and became trusted neighbors. Ed was Shead Memorial High School's vice principal, having been on the faculty for nineteen years. He graciously helped our transition to teaching. Lillian's passion was cooking; Ed's was Atlantic salmon fishing—the "sport of kings"—on the nearby Dennys River. Ed was so accomplished at fly fishing that the legendary Ted Williams, the Boston Red Sox outfielder, became his regular fishing partner and friend. Ed caught the salmon, Lillian cooked them, and we ate them.

Green Peas with a Purpose

While Suzanne and I had no intention of becoming career educators, we were committed to teaching with excellence. The state of Maine gave us temporary teaching credentials, because they couldn't entice anyone to teach in Eastport. It was the Californians or no one.

We were pea green teachers in need of a lot of coaching.

Fortunately, Gene Wilbur was our principal. He must have cringed when we reported to his office. We were twenty-one years old, and a few of our students were second-year seniors, nineteen years old. Even worse, we looked like two malnourished high school students. But Mr. Wilbur (we never called him Gene) guided us though a rough first month. He was a tall, powerfully built man, with wrists so large he couldn't button his sleeves. He would have made a formidable football or hockey player.

Before school started, Mr. Wilbur gave us a pep talk, anticipating student behavioral problems. "Just remember," he said, "If you have a student get out of control and send him or her to me, you will be giving away your authority. It will become more difficult to correct them next time." We rarely kicked problem students in his direction, finding creative ways to control the classroom.

About 200 students and thirteen teachers were shoehorned into Shead Memorial High School, a two-story brick building from another era. The basement housed an ancient boiler that generally kept the building too hot—but made an ideal retreat for one of the teachers to drink. A modern gym was adjacent to the main building, home of the town's pride and joy, the Tiger basketball team. Schools in Down East Maine were too small and poor to support a football team, so basketball reigned supreme. I volunteered to coach junior varsity basketball, and Suzanne sponsored the JV cheerleaders. I also assisted the varsity coach, Kendrick Mitchell. Kendrick and I worked well together—we only clashed over his loyalty to the Boston Celtics and mine to the Los Angeles Lakers.

Helen's Restaurant

Shortly after moving to Eastport, we began searching for a church. Most church congregations in Eastport were quite small, aging, in decline. So we decided to look for a church in another town, which also offered us more personal privacy. We liked the seaside town of Machias—45 miles down scenic Highway 1—in part because it was home to the best seafood restaurant in New England: Helen's. We reasoned that if we attended church and then ate the seafood platter (heavy on the lobster) and Maine blueberry pie at Helen's Restaurant, our Sundays would be complete.

But was there a church for our needs? After some research, we discovered the Machias Valley Baptist Church. Neither of us had ever attended a Baptist church, but they appeared to have a lively congregation. Our first Sunday was encouraging, though we didn't eat at Helen's that day. Pastor George Henderson and his wife Carolyn invited us to lunch at their home. For the remainder of the school year, the church and Helen's became our Sunday retreat.

Macbeth for a Motley Group

The first four months were a challenge, especially for Suzanne. In addition to French, she taught English and supervised a study hall. Study hall—I had one too—at times got out of control. The students tested us, because we were "from away" (anyone not born in Eastport was from away), we talked differently (to them I was "Mis-tah Spring-ah"), and we looked younger than a few of them. This was a difficult situation, but we were determined to make the best of it. Once they knew we meant business and weren't going to back down, the two sides formed an uneasy truce.

Suzanne was assigned perhaps the most difficult class in the school: Senior General English Literature, composed of eleven boys and two girls who had absolutely no interest in English or literature. They were the school troublemakers, the students the rest of the faculty had given up on. Several of them were nineteen years old.

The school textbooks were out-of-date, worn, and irrelevant. In desperation, Suzanne approached Mr. Wilbur and asked if she could do something different with her class. "I'd like to study Shakespeare's *Macbeth* for the entire semester." He approved, and the class jumped into a story that included prophecy, witches, political ambition, murders, and intrigue. In retrospect, *Macbeth* was perfect for this motley group.

What started as a class in rebellion turned into a group of students excited about learning. Later in the fall, Suzanne was called out of class on JV cheerleader business. There was no substitute teacher, so upon returning Suzanne feared the worst. Instead, she discovered the class had elected fellow student Lester Pulk teacher, and he was leading an informed discussion on the play. This remains one of Suzanne's dearest compliments.

As fall turned to winter, the days shortened and got considerably colder. During the northern winter, we drove to school in the dark and returned home in the dark. Being on an island, temperatures were moderated by the Bay of Fundy, and the salt air melted snow accumulations. For that we were grateful.

"Oh God, Oh God, Oh God"

Down East life wasn't all gloom and freezing temperatures. In early October we slipped away to Baxter State Park and Mount Katahdin to enjoy spectacular peak foliage—burgundy reds, lemon yellows, pumpkin oranges.

At Thanksgiving break Suzanne and I drove through northern Maine to Quebec City in Canada, where we escaped to a romantic ski resort, and where everyone spoke French. Suzanne felt at home. The skiing was perfect, and the food memorable—especially the flaming cherry crepes jubilee, which we talk about with watering mouths to this day. This Canadian trip was our second honeymoon.

On the drive to Quebec City we were reminded that our lives are in God's hands. Ninety percent of Maine is forested, and the isolated road to Quebec was heavily trafficked by ubiquitous logging trucks. A short distance before the Canadian border we drove onto a two-lane highway covered with black ice. We had no warning nor control over the car; chugging uphill toward us was a fully loaded logging truck. Braking or steering only made things worse, so we picked up a head of steam and headed straight at the truck for which Kirschen was no match. Our prayer was uncomplicated: "Oh God, Oh God, Oh God" We might have added, "We're gonna die!" Then the hand of God came down, gently moved our Cortina to the right, and we screamed past death.

The Quebec getaway put us in a good mood to face the December 1 draft lottery for the highly unpopular Viet Nam war. Every draft-eligible male was entered in a lottery based on his birthday; the Selective Service drew numbers in ascending order. The lower the number, the higher the probability of being called up. Suzanne kept a copy of the letter she wrote home on December 2:

> Well, well, what a night! We (at least I) went through such different emotions during that drawing—calmness, shock, panic, fear, FRUSTRATION, trust; mostly trust, but it was something else. We had listened to the first 60 or so numbers on one radio station, then switched stations to where they were announcing as they drew. Here we joined in at number 120, not knowing if Kevin's number had been called in between. So, on we listened until number 254: October 16.

Number 254 was considered high enough not to be called up. Suzanne continues:

> You know, I knew the Lord had given us this year together, but I really didn't know what He wanted for us after that. The only way I thought He might keep Kevin out is that He has given us such a strong and beautiful love for one another—a love so great that it

really pains us to be apart even for a few hours. And when I think of how He gave us His love, it does seem likely that He would keep us together. But we are only humans of inferior minds and don't have an inkling of how His great mind works, so all we can do is trust his superior wisdom and planning.

There is a reason why Kevin was given such a late number. The Lord wants us to do something else other than the army, so we must keep tuned in to his will. Oh, Blessed Lord.

Pappy and Uncle Andy

At Christmas break we flew down to Florida to visit my grandfather Pappy and Uncle Andy. They had moved to Coral Gables for health reasons, where they opened a dry-cleaning business. After we endured a circuitous flight on soon to be bankrupt Northeast Airlines, Uncle Andy welcomed us to his "world famous" chicken and dumplings dinner.

The warm weather and sunshine were a welcome relief from the winter cold and darkness of Maine.

Rosie, their sole employee, spent a lot of time at their home. She and Uncle Andy seemed to hit it off. We thought they made a great couple, so Suzanne hatched a plan: Why don't Uncle Andy and Rosie get married? We approached Uncle Andy with the idea, and he graciously said he would think about it. We loved Uncle Andy, and he adored Suzanne. He was a kind-hearted man.

The next year we visited my older brother, a naval aviator living in Maryland, and excitedly shared our Uncle Andy-Rosie marriage plan. "And there's an extra room in the house that would be perfect for Pappy!"

Robin patiently listened, looking back and forth at us. I suspected something was wrong. Then he said, "Are you finished?" With satisfied grins we both said, "Yes!"

Then he said, "What turnip truck did you two just fall off? They are homosexuals. Pappy and Uncle Andy are a homosexual couple." With that he threw up his hands, stood up, and walked away.

We sat in silence for a few moments, looked at each other, and suddenly it made perfect sense. And we felt like we had just fallen off a turnip truck. We have laughed at our naivete ever since.

The Battle Begins

After Christmas in Coral Gables we returned to our teaching jobs, refreshed and confident about finishing well at Shead Memorial High School. I was looking forward to the basketball season, especially instilling the Johnny Wooden philosophy of aggressive, full-court press play I learned at Paul Revere Junior High School and Palisades High School.

Meanwhile in Suzanne's Senior General English Literature class, Vaughn Pottle turned in a test with a peace sign at the top. After correcting the test, she wrote next to his grade, "If you want to know real peace, come talk to me sometime." Vaughn approached her a few days later in study hall, and she arranged for him to visit us one evening in our little home on Clark Street. He showed up, and I shared the gospel with him. Much to our shock, he got on his knees, repented of his sin, and committed his life to Christ.

Vaughn's life was transformed. He went from a major behavior problem and D student to cooperative and an A student. Vaughn was bright and an influencer. Other students saw the changes and began asking questions. He was vocal. "It's all about Jesus!"

Suzanne and I proposed sponsoring a weekly voluntary, lunch-hour Bible study at school, focusing on Paul's letter to the Ephesians. Vaughn would get the word out to the students. We innocently thought it was no big deal.

Before our first Bible study at school, Mr. Wilbur called us into his office. He said we had the legal right to sponsor a voluntary Bible study, but he asked that we not do it on campus. Unbeknownst to us, he was receiving pressure from the community, including several staff members. We respected Mr. Wilbur and didn't want to create more problems for him, so we agreed and opened our home.

In Eastport, everyone knew everybody's business, which meant they knew our business. They even had a network for passing along gossip: the milkman. The milkman home delivered non-homogenized milk in glass bottles—thick cream rose to the top; yummy—on the front porch, twice a week. He was nicknamed by locals the "Midnight Milkman." As he made deliveries house to house, he was frequently invited in for coffee and the latest chatter. Sometimes there were so many rumors to pass along he did not finish his route until midnight. We were destined to become a frequent topic on his moonlit route.

When I announced the weekly Bible study was moving to our home, interest exploded. After a couple of weeks, rumors abounded on the Midnight Milkman's route. One rumor was that I was not qualified to teach the Bible because I hadn't gone to seminary or Bible college; the other rumor was that this was an orgy with Suzanne. But God doesn't waste anything, even tarnished reputations.

Gossip only made the Bible study more attractive to students. I call it the forbidden-fruit syndrome; teenagers want to do what their parents disapprove of. God used parental resistance to bring more kids to the study and into his kingdom.

At the height of the controversy, I awakened early one morning and looked out our front window to see a charred and blackened cross and crown of thorns planted in our front yard. Our car also was vandalized, though not seriously damaged. The town was sending a message.

As gossip spread, fellow teachers started talking. When either Suzanne or I walked in the smoke-filled teachers' lounge, all talking would cease. We tried to be people of integrity, honorable, respectful, and hard-working. But we were "from away" and thus suspect, and we were speaking up for Christ. As the semester progressed, and it became obvious this was merely a Bible study and Suzanne was not conducting orgies, our colleagues softened.

A few weeks after we started the study, and more students turned to Christ, I was contacted by the local ministers' association. They asked permission to send an official representative to the Bible study to check us out. "Sure," I said. "We'd be honored to have you."

The night the Congregational minister showed up the room was packed, but we gave him a comfortable seat. The evening went well. He didn't say a word, though he was cordial. Later he told the town's religious leaders, "It's a Bible study, nothing more." And just like that, the controversy lost its steam.

Baby Booties

In April, Suzanne suspected she might be pregnant, so she made an appointment with Eastport's only physician, Dr. French. In those days, a sample had to be sent to Boston to determine pregnancy or not, and that took about two weeks. The results came back positive; only Suzanne, Dr. French, his nurse, and I knew. Suzanne and I quietly celebrated, and phoned home on a pay phone—we had no land line—to share our secret joy. A few weeks later at a local church bazaar fundraiser Suzanne scrutinized the knitted items, which included baby booties. The unknown woman behind the table chimed, "I guess you will be needing some of those soon." No doubt the news had already passed through the Midnight Milkman's route.

Suzanne was furious about the lack of confidentiality; the leak only could have come from the doctor's office. Then she realized, hey, it's a small town. By the end of the school year, when it was out in the open that Suzanne was expecting, a group of teachers and students gave her a baby shower, a kind and touching event. All was forgiven.

The last two months in Eastport were uneventful. As the weather warmed up and the days lengthened, we were thinking about departing. A couple of weeks before school was out, Mr. Wilbur called us into his office and informed us that the school board was inviting us to return the next year. We were surprised but concluded Mr. Wilbur likely was behind the offer.

We declined. Our Eastport adventure was coming to an end. Our plan was to drive to Mansfield and spend a few nights in housing provided by the ministry center, and then head home to San Diego or Santa Barbara.

But we were to learn once again that our plans are rarely God's plans.

FIVE

In the School of Discipleship

Mansfield, Ohio

*"The most important thing in your life
is not what you do; it's who you become.
That's what you will take into eternity."*
—Dallas Willard, *Soul Keeping*

S hortly before leaving Eastport to return home to California, I got a severe toothache. Ed Bartlett referred me to his dentist—"the best dentist in Maine"—in Ellsworth, a town one hundred miles down the coast, inland from Bar Harbor. This same tooth, a molar, had landed me in a dentist's chair in Arrowhead, California, on our honeymoon. The molar had deteriorated since then, now needing an expensive root canal and gold crown. Total cost: $1,000.

Our combined annual incomes were $11,000, and we had earmarked our last $1,000 to pay for the 3,500-mile return trip across America. We were flat broke.

Determined to stand on our own feet, we were unwilling to ask our parents for a loan. Our plans needed to be altered. Ray Nethery had extended free housing at the Grace Haven Ministry Center in Ohio. I reasoned I could get a temporary job for a few weeks, we could then drive home, have our baby, and pursue God's calling for our lives.

Proverbs 16:9 says, "The heart of man plans his way, but the Lord establishes his steps." Having given me a sore tooth and emptied our bank account, God was about to maroon us in a town and state in which we did not want to live.

But he had bigger plans for us.

Obedience Check

When we arrived in Mansfield, Ray asked us if we had received a letter from him before leaving Eastport. "No." "Well," he said, "We are inviting you to serve on staff here at Grace Haven. Our focus is two-fold. First, a discipleship and evangelism ministry to college students patterned off Francis Schaeffer's L'Abri in Switzerland, and second, planting churches." L'Abri is a Swiss community founded in 1955 by Francis and Edith Schaeffer. Francis Schaeffer was a theologian and philosopher who wrote many influential books on Christian apologetics. At L'Abri—meaning "the shelter" in French—young people sought answers to honest questions about God and the significance of life.

We didn't know how to respond to Ray's invitation, so we said we'd pray about it.

Unsure about our immediate future, we sublet the apartment of a young couple who were away for the summer. I started looking for a job, still thinking we were returning to California. That was our plan.

During this time, I received a Big Word: God was calling me to full-time ministry, but we needed to trust him for specifics. This Big Word came during prayer, when I knew deep within my soul—the Holy Spirit frequently works that way—telling me I needed to take a big risk with God, one step at a time. Suzanne wholeheartedly agreed—we were called by God to serve together.

The first big step in my calling was to accept the position at Grace Haven. We were attracted to the idealism of Christian community, discipleship, building theological foundations, and character formation.

In obedience to God's Big Word, we accepted the invitation to join staff—knowing little of the details. At that point in our adventure, we wanted to serve and learn. Had we foreseen how difficult it would be, we might not have accepted.

Immediate Temptation

Shortly after agreeing to join staff, I went to the local State Farm Insurance agency to transfer my auto policy. The agent was unusually inquisitive, asking all sorts of personal questions about my family: how long Suzanne and I had been married, where I grew up, where I attended university. Finally, I cut the conversation short, completed my business, and went on my way. A second agent, a gray-haired man, was sitting at a desk nearby and appeared to be eavesdropping on our conversation.

Later that afternoon, I received a call from the gray-haired agent who introduced himself and asked if he could visit Suzanne and me at our home in the morning. "I already have life insurance," I said.

"I promise you I'm not trying to sell life insurance or any other type of insurance." He was insistent the meeting be in our home.

I didn't believe he wasn't trying to sell something, but our morning was open, and we were curious. "Okay, we are available at nine o'clock in the morning."

When we met, he immediately started asking personal questions. The meeting felt like a job interview, although he shared a little about himself. He was from Columbus, a regional manager with State Farm. Finally, after an hour, Suzanne asked, "What is this all about?"

"Well, the man who built the agency you were in yesterday recently left his wife and ran off to Florida with his secretary. He abandoned the agency and left a significant client base. I am here to offer you the business, with a sizable starting annual salary. I have confidence that you will quickly be making substantially more than that, and you will be a wealthy man by the time you are in your thirties. This is a unique situation. I have never done anything like this in my career." If I had accepted the offer and worked hard, we might have been secure financially for the rest of our lives. The salary wasn't too little, I concluded, but the cost to my calling was too high.

Within days of saying yes to God's Big Word for me, we received a generous offer of material riches. We could not accept the State Farm job, because God had other plans for our lives. The agent was dumbfounded, repeating he had never offered anything like this to anyone. He pleaded with us, but we told him that we had to obey God's call for our lives. Big Words, life altering words, are almost always tested.

Eric Liddell, who won a Gold Medal in the 1924 Olympics and whose track career was immortalized in the 1981 film *Chariots of Fire*, wrote, "Ask yourself: if I know something to be true, am I prepared to follow it, even though it is contrary to what I want, or to what I previously held to be true? Will I follow it if it means being laughed at, if it means personal financial loss, or some kind of hardship?" This was one of those times.

When you say "yes" to God, life often does not get easier. I turned down financial security for the uncertainty of an adventure with God.

Life in Community

Grace Haven was a 400-acre farm in North-Central Ohio, donated by Hod Bolesky, a wealthy industrialist. The student ministry was built around three or four "householder" families, each with a separate home. Eventually there was a lodge with multiple meeting rooms, a library, and an institutional kitchen. The householders were expected to house young adults and host rotating "farm dinners" for the students living at Grace Haven. Meal participants varied between 20 and 30 people, depending on the time of year. For our first few years, Suzanne and I hosted farm dinners every three days.

Our salary wasn't close to what State Farm offered. It was zero. We were expected to raise our own income. We would never make over $11,000 annually during our seven-year tenure at Grace Haven. In 1974 our adjusted gross income was $7,400—equivalent in purchasing power to about $40,000 today. Housing was provided, though not the utilities, and the working farm supplied much of our food but not all. Homes were large, with room for up to a dozen overnight guests.

Hudson Taylor, the founder of China Inland Mission, once said, "The Lord's work done in the Lord's way will never fail to have the Lord's provision." This is supposed to be an encouraging word that many pastors and missionaries learn early in their ministry. But I thought, "Well, that might have worked for Hudson Taylor, but I'm no Hudson Taylor. Help!" I struggled with insecurity and fear that I would fail to adequately care for my young family. Money, or the lack of it, would be my greatest concern during our Mansfield years.

However, despite my lack of faith, we never missed a meal, nor did any of our guests. We always had enough money to live, though rarely any to save. Perhaps the most remarkable aspect of teetering on the edge financially was Suzanne's faith and confidence that God would meet our needs. She neither complained nor wavered in trusting God. This was especially remarkable because she was raised with money to spare. Suzanne was a model of dependency on Christ, practicing contentment and wise stewardship. She lived by the words of Augustine: "Pray as though everything depended on God. Work as though everything depended on you." Every morning she trusted God anew, then looked for the best sales and smartest buys. And the most strategic places to give; her generosity knows no bounds. Suzanne's faith covered my unbelief, which fulfilled Paul's words, "We who are strong have an obligation to bear with the failings of the weak and not to please ourselves" (Romans 15:1). In the area of personal finances, she was and remains my leader.

The college students, coming from as far as California and Europe, were frequently on interim semesters. They worked half-day on the farm—in artisan shops, the dairy barn or vegetable gardens, in a bookstore—and in householders' kitchens helping the wives prepare the evening meals.

The students were Christians, atheists, seekers, hippies, artists, musicians, druggies, lost. They were chaotic at times, but never boring. They all had questions—many questions about life, death, God, drugs, the Bible, truth, meaning.

Jeep, Joyce, Hans, and Marilyn

We also occasionally hosted young hitchhikers—common in those days—who showed up on our doorsteps. One person stands out in my mind, "Jeep," a recently returned Vietnam War veteran so named because he drove jeeps in the war. I never learned his true name. Jeep was a broken man, probably suffering from PTSD, but like everyone who came to Grace Haven, God brought him into our lives. He was, without question, one of the most frustrating people I ever ministered to. I asked him to work afternoons in one of our artisan shops, and I tried in vain to oversee his morning studies and discussions. When he left Grace Haven after a few months, I felt both relieved and a failure.

But Jeep taught me an important truth. My calling is to love the people God brings into my life, to witness the truth of his grace, and to mediate the hope of eternal life. And God, through his Spirit, works his truth into their lives in ways that I cannot see. Long after Jeep left Grace Haven, I received an email from someone who's name I didn't recognize, saying, "Kevin, I wanted to write you to say what you did for me and said to me twenty-five years ago had a profound effect on my life. You knew me as Jeep in those days. I am now a committed Christian living in New Jersey, married to a wonderful Christian woman and have great kids. I know I frustrated you at Grace Haven, but you planted the seeds that led me to a relationship with Christ." As Paul wrote to the Corinthians, "Neither he who plants nor he who waters is anything, but only God who gives the growth" (1 Corinthians 3:7).

Not all the Grace Haven stories had as happy an ending as Jeep's. Joyce, a non-religious university student from the East Coast, came for an interim semester. She was perhaps the most troubled student in our tenure. Suzanne took her under her wing, loving her, listening to her, praying for her. Joyce was bright but deeply alienated from her parents. On Mother's Day, 1975, I insisted Suzanne and I and our two children spend a day alone as a family enjoying the tulips at Kingwood Center. Suzanne was quite concerned for Joyce, knowing Mother's Day could be difficult for her. Upon returning home that afternoon, we saw emergency vehicles outside the lodge; Joyce had taken her life. When her parents came to receive her remains, they were irritated that their daughter's suicide interrupted their European vacation.

Many students taught me more than I taught them. Hans Bayer was a German whose father served under Hitler in World War II. Hans helped me to understand the depth and high cost of evil of Nazi Germany. We were only 30 years removed from the war; our discussions about it were intense, and Hans was insightful. One observation stuck with me. He said his father's post-war generation was under a dark cloud of condemnation. "When they held a gun aimed at an innocent person, they had a choice to pull the trigger or drop the gun and die with the victims. They rarely made the righteous choice." Hans eventually earned a PhD in theology from the University of Aberdeen in Scotland and taught for many years at Concordia Seminary in St. Louis. He chose righteousness.

Grace Haven is also where Suzanne and I counseled our first married couple in crisis. We were twenty-four years old when Ray asked us to meet with a couple from Tennessee who were considering divorce. They were twenty-two years old and recently graduated from college. He had been a star athlete and she a beauty queen, but they knew little about marriage. We listened to them, prayed for them, directed them to scripture, and encouraged them. We also felt completely out of our league, but God used our words and they decided to pursue reconciliation. A few years ago, we heard from mutual friends that they were still married and have raised five children.

Then there was Marilyn. She was taking a semester off from an Ivy League school, coming to Grace Haven to investigate the claims of Christianity. Marilyn had a unique problem: She could not say the name of Jesus. Literally. She could not utter the word, "Jesus." She frequently worked with Suzanne making farm dinners, sharing her struggles. Suzanne proposed we pray with her one evening, and that is when something happened that we had only read about in the Bible. After she described her inability to say the name of Jesus, we suggested prayer. When we started to pray, she fell off her chair onto the floor, saying blasphemous words against God in a frightening voice and giving off a horrible smell.

We were shocked and frightened, not knowing what to do at first. Then I thought, well, why not do what Paul in the book of Acts did when encountering a demonized girl: "In the name of Jesus Christ I command you to come out of her!" (Acts 16:18). We knew we did not have authority in ourselves over evil spirits, but Christ defeated Satan at the cross. So, we prayed, "We command you evil spirits to stop talking," and she became quiet. Then we prayed, "In the name of Jesus, come out of Marilyn," and they came out. Marilyn's eyes cleared; she sat up and said she could not remember anything that had just happened. Then we said, "Marilyn, say the name of Jesus," and she did—for the first time in her life. We shared the gospel with her, and she prayed to receive Christ. Marilyn still had problems to work through—she was an abuse victim—but now she could receive counseling and begin the process of emotional healing and discipleship.

Uncertainty and Insecurity

Our first home at Grace Haven was a large, run-down, one-hundred-year-old farmhouse, with pipes that frequently froze in the winter. A barn that had seen better days was across our driveway and home to a hundred chickens—Ray assigned their care to me. You could say my first flock was a hundred chickens. The good news was we were supplied with unlimited eggs; the bad news was my daily responsibilities included their feeding, watering, cleaning the coops (chickens are filthy), egg collection, and delivery to other householders.

We were 2,000 miles from home, poor, and pregnant. The only job I could find was working part-time as a lawn and garden equipment salesman in a Montgomery Ward department store. This lasted three months. Then I operated chair lifts at Snow Trails, the local ski resort, which would not qualify as a bunny hill in California. But I made enough to keep food on the table and squeeze in ministry time with students at Grace Haven.

Uncertainty and insecurity colored our first year in Mansfield. Shortly after joining staff, a disagreement arose between the two directors, Ray Nethery and Gordon Walker. Gordon was a Baptist pastor from Tennessee, recently serving as Ohio State University's Campus Crusade Director. They had different personalities, leadership styles, and philosophies of ministry. Gordon thought the farm should be a conference center; Ray's vision was for a community patterned off L'Abri, which was the primary attraction for Suzanne and me.

Breaking Ice

Gordon Walker was an excellent Bible teacher, and a group in Nashville pledged financial support for him and his family if they moved back to Tennessee. He accepted their invitation. Ray may have won the day, but he was left with a wounded puppy—a ministry divided between followers attracted to different leadership philosophies. As such, Ray carefully and with sensitivity exercised authority to bring focus and unity to Grace Haven. "Leadership," Ray told me, "is more an art than a technology. We are caring for image bearers of God, who deserve respect and patience as we mediate Christ's presence to them."

During his brief tenure before he moved, Gordon and I had rarely interacted, but he did create a memorable ministry moment for me. One freezing January weekend, a group of Ohio State University students attended a conference at the farm. The lodge had not been built, so the students crammed into a meeting room in Gordon's large basement. On Saturday night he preached from Mark 16:16 ("Whoever believes and is baptized will be saved . . .") and at least half a dozen students committed their lives to Christ. Being a good Baptist, Gordon said, "Now you need to be baptized!"

But where? There was only one place: the small swimming pond covered with a thin layer of ice, about seventy-five yards below his home. The new believers enthusiastically said, "Let's do it!" Then Gordon announced, "Yes! And our new staffer, Kevin Springer, will baptize you." The group schussed through the snow to the pond, and I shivered into the water, creating a channel of broken ice in my wake. Then with full immersion I baptized them in the name of the Father, Son, and Holy Spirit. That night I learned ice water numbs the human body so quickly you cannot feel anything. Remarkably, not one of us got ill.

A Nobody for Jesus

That winter of 1970, I took stock of my life. By passing up medical school or graduate school in marine biology and the State Farm job,

I had walked away from a secure and comfortable future. And, for what? Cleaning chicken coops, selling lawn and garden equipment in the winter at Montgomery Ward in Mansfield, Ohio, and housing and feeding a steady stream of strangers. Oh, and my wife was eight months pregnant.

Henry David Thoreau wrote, "If I seem not to keep in step with others, it is because I am listening to another drumbeat." God was teaching me that he did not need my talents and abilities; he only wanted my attention and availability. He wanted me to hear his drumbeat. My ambition and pride had to die. "Without me," Jesus said in John 15, "you can do nothing."

Mary Healy remarked on Jesus' calling of four fishermen in Mark 1: "Following Jesus means a break with the past and a willingness to let go of all other attachments. Not everyone is called literally to abandon their profession or family, but all are called to put everything in second priority to him. Saying yes to that call is the first step in a lifelong adventure."

I was no longer a hot shot from Malibu, I was a nobody serving in Mansfield. God had Suzanne and me right where he wanted us, in the school of discipleship.

My real training program was in my heart, where God was testing me. The problem with Big Words is sometimes they put you where you don't want to be, doing what you don't want to do. Did I question his direction for our life? No. Did I like it? No.

Amid our testing came one of the biggest blessings of our lives: The birth of our first child, Kelley Noelle, on December 24, 1970. Everything about her birth was an act of grace. Suzanne's obstetrician, Doug Veach, waived his fee. A massive snowstorm hit Ohio the day Kelley was born, but we drove sixty miles down I-71 to St. Ann's Hospital in Columbus with no incident. Suzanne, who looked like a toothpick with an olive in the middle, had a normal birth. Returning home with Kelley snuggled in a big red Christmas stocking supplied by the hospital, the world looked different. We were a family with a great future full of hope. Kelley's bassinet was our converted sweater drawer. Everything was perfect.

Happy mom and dad with baby Kelley

Another Move

When Gordon moved to Tennessee, Suzanne and I moved into his recently built and beautiful home, overlooking a picturesque red barn, idyllic meadow, and the spring-fed pond in which I had baptized students. The generous basement housed up to ten female students in two large dorm rooms, and a meeting room. The converted garage became a guest wing for hosting special visitors.

I bid farewell to my hundred chickens. I didn't miss them.

We would not have lasted six months at Grace Haven without Suzanne's gift of hospitality, welcoming anyone and everyone who entered our home. She opened her heart and spirit, and I followed along. Indefatigable in body, mind, and soul, she pressed forward, dragging me along when I wanted to give up. We were a team, but it came at a cost; hospitality always costs something. Suzanne writes,

Among the lovely wedding presents Kevin and I had been given was a beautiful, carved crystal vase. We hauled that to Maine and then down to Mansfield, Ohio. When we moved into the 100-year-old farmhouse, we needed to supply some of the furnishings. For the couple's bedroom, I had found an antique dresser and vanity. Not having any bedside tables, I used our TV tray tables, the metal-leg kind. A bit wobbly, they had to suffice.

One of our first guests was a young married couple, and I wanted the room to be welcoming. Finding lovely wildflowers, I placed them in the crystal vase and set that on the TV tray.

Not long after the couple occupied the room, a loud crash echoed throughout the downstairs. Rather casually, but apologizing, the wife came to me and said the vase got knocked onto the floor and broke. I had a split second to steady myself and say, "That's okay, the tray table was wobbly in the first place." Part of me wanted to say, "Do you know that was crystal, not just glass, and a wedding present to boot?" But of course, that would have been terrible on my part. I am so glad that in that instant the Holy Spirit gave me the proper attitude.

This was my first lesson of acknowledging that (1) everything we have belongs to God anyway, and we are mere stewards; and (2) people matter way more than things.

Suzanne and I settled into our new home, focusing on community, discipling young students, and rearing baby Kelley. Francis Schaeffer's teachings helped me to know what I believe and why I believe it, and to effectively communicate and defend the gospel.

In 1971, Ray asked me to write a letter on behalf of the ministry, requesting a building variance to the Richland County Zoning Board. Hod Bolesky had agreed to build a lodge to accommodate the flourishing student ministry and a new church building. Under protest, I wrote the letter. "You're asking somebody who can't write to write." But he saw something in me that I could not see. Ray surprised me when he said an influential zoning board member was opposed to the lodge until she read my letter, which she described as compelling and convincing.

That day I heard God's still small voice: "You will be a writer." Only later did I recognize it as a Big Word. Not long after, I was editing *Commonlife*, a magazine for evangelicals concerning Christian community, spiritual renewal, and the advance of Christian truth. As editor I attended annual Evangelical Press Association meetings, where I networked with publishers and editors in the Christian periodical publishing industry. I interviewed authors like Elisabeth Elliot, Peter Kreeft, Paul Vitz, Os Guinness, and a variety of Christian artists. I also started the Grace Haven Book Store, which broadened my knowledge of the Christian book publishing industry.

On Easter Sunday, April 22, 1973, our son, Shad Mathew, was born. Our family was growing, and we were settling into a rhythm of life that included meaning, ministry, and community. Our finances weren't getting any better, but our needs were met every month.

Suzanne riding near the pond below our home where I baptized Ohio State University students

Kicking against the Goads

Suzanne and I were a team; when God spoke Big Words to me or her, we pursued them together. When we agreed to become householders, Suzanne took on a tremendous burden. She, too, had obedience tests, perhaps the biggest in 1971. Here is her story, in her words:

The work at Grace Haven was intense. Every three days I was responsible for preparing and hosting a meal for twenty-plus people in our home. The other two days were devoted to normal household and mothering tasks, meal planning, and grocery shopping.

Kevin and I secretly wanted out. This just seemed too much. Even after already giving up pursuing medical school two years earlier, now that seemed a viable alternative. Columbus, Ohio, was a great city with a medical school. In my mind, I pictured a tree-lined street with us living in a little home, picket fence and all. Of course, I had no idea how we could afford school or rent a home, but I kept that image in my mind for about six months, using the strong possibility of this being our future to help me survive the present.

When Kevin completed his medical school applications, he put them in stamped envelopes and headed off to mail them. But once again he had an overwhelming sense that this was not God's will for us. He told me he couldn't go against what God was telling him. He threw the applications in the trash. My fantasy world came crashing down. My dreams were crushed.

Bitterly disappointed in God, I walked up our staircase and collapsed on the first landing. I cried out to God, 'If you are not going to change our circumstances, you have to change me to be able to live with them.'

A simple prayer of surrender. A beat-down prayer of surrender, but God takes us at our word. In the next weeks and years, he strengthened me to stay and serve, even giving me joy.

Suzanne and community members preparing for a farm dinner

When Paul was converted on the road to Damascus, he heard a Big Word from God: "Saul, Saul, why are you persecuting me? It is hard for you to kick against the goads." Goads were long, sharpened sticks used to prod oxen when they were hitched to yokes. The ox would kick against the sticks, but they soon learned it was better to accept the direction of the farmer than "kick against the goad." It is foolish and futile to resist God's will.

Seminary

Shortly after the birth of our son, Ray Nethery suggested I enroll at Ashland Theological Seminary (ATS), a twenty-minute drive up I-71 toward Cleveland. He felt I needed deeper theological foundations—a critical building block to knowing what I believe and why I believe it. "But Ray," I said, "I don't have the money to pay tuition. I have two children to feed, and every three nights another twenty to thirty people."

Ray responded, "God will provide." He was correct.

Seminary would not have happened without the generosity of ATS Dean Joseph Schultz. At that time ATS was in decline, struggling to attract new students. When Dean Schultz learned I was a University of Southern California graduate he cut a deal with me. "If you let me feature you in our literature to attract new students, I will give you a full scholarship."

At ATS, two men had a profound influence in my life. The first was the Old Testament and Theology Professor Joseph Kickasola, who introduced me to the writings of George Eldon Ladd, especially his *Gospel of the Kingdom* and *A Theology of the New Testament*. Dr. Kickasola grounded me in Reformed theology.

The other influence came from Owen Alderfer, my church history professor, who taught me an appreciation for and understanding of the depth and breadth of historical theology, especially the writings of Augustine, John Calvin, Martin Luther, and Jonathan Edwards—and other church fathers. Dr. Alderfer, whom I consider one of my mentors, challenged me to find beauty and grace in all orthodox Christian traditions. His humility and integrity modeled the kind of man I wanted to become. I served as his teaching assistant my last year.

I did well academically at ATS, earning an M.A. in May of 1976 with a focus in church history and historical theology. A year after graduating, Dean Schultz, at Dr. Alderfer's recommendation, proposed I pursue a PhD in History, with emphasis on Reformation and Renaissance History, and return to the seminary as a church history professor when Dr. Alderfer retired in a few years. Their offer was tempting, something to pray about.

Word and Spirit

In 1 John 2:14, the Apostle John writes, "I am writing to you, young men, because you are strong, and the word of God abides in you, and you have overcome the evil one." By 1975, God had built significant biblical foundations in me—core biblical truth that all Christians for all time have believed. As John says, God expects the word of God to "abide" in young men (and women), which means it lives in them, transforming their innermost parts. I don't worship the Bible; I worship the Triune God who is revealed in the Bible—a relationship understood in light of the illuminating and searching power of the Holy Spirit. As I took hold of God's word, it took hold of me—penetrating my conscience, will—even "the thoughts and intentions of [my] heart" (Hebrews 4:12).

By 1975, Ray recognized I was willing, even liked, to take risks. Big adventures bring greater rewards; and when you fail, you learn how to do it better next time. Ray gave me a new assignment. "We've had students from several small, private Ohio colleges come to Grace Haven. Contact them, go to their campuses, network, evangelize, disciple and train, and help build student groups that impact their campuses for Christ." Ray recognized gifts of teaching, evangelism, and leadership in me—specifically the willingness to start new ministries. Now was the time for risk taking, trusting the Holy Spirit to fill me with faith and lead to ripe fields for harvest.

For the next couple of years, I built relationships at the College of Wooster, Case Western Reserve, and Cleveland State University. I failed to make any connection at Cleveland State, and taught a short-lived Bible study to nursing students at Case Western Reserve. I settled into the College of Wooster, a small, Presbyterian school with outstanding academics, forming a deep connection with student leaders Stuart Brown, and his future wife, Peggy Frank.

I learned through success and failure. Cleveland State was a commuter school, making it difficult to form meaningful relationships with students. Contacts at Case Western Reserve were all women, more appropriately evangelized by women. The College of Wooster was residential and co-educational, a perfect environment to evangelize and disciple young people, especially young men.

Ordination

On March 11, 1977, I was ordained. Ray Nethery, Jon Braun, Gordon Walker, and Mike Seiler laid hands on me after I took my vows. Jon Braun said, "Kevin, this is the second time I have stood before you as a judge. The last time I did I said, 'Kevin, will you take Suzanne to be your wedded wife, and do you promise and covenant before God and these witnesses to be her loving and faithful husband…' and you responded affirmatively. Every bit as seriously I address similarly to you tonight a charge, as Ray will ask you in a brief time for a response every bit as serious and every bit as affirmative as the one you gave me then."

Ray then called for four affirmations: To teach orthodox, sound doctrine; To stand with the catholic (universal) church; To serving leadership; To be submitted to God and fear him. I responded "yes" to all four questions—before God and the witnesses—and have endeavored to fulfill my vows in the power of the Holy Spirit for the rest of my life.

Two Kingdoms

During my Grace Haven years two experiences, one of heaven and the other of hell, profoundly affected me. They are both difficult to describe. In the first, I experienced a taste of heaven on earth while worshipping God with 200 members of our local church. We were praising God in song—I don't remember the song—when suddenly I was overcome by God's presence and a remarkable harmony of heart and mind with my brothers and sisters. I can only describe it as a tiny foretaste of what eternity will be like. It was like heaven came to earth, and with one voice we worshipped the Triune God for who he is—perfect grace, beauty, power, accessibility. Lasting only a few minutes, yet touching on eternity, I saw, felt, and experienced God in a way that made this life seem ephemeral. In those few minutes I had a preview of the fulness of the kingdom of God.

I have never had a corporate worship experience of that magnitude since, but that foretaste of the new heavens and earth is enough to keep me keeping on in this world.

The second experience was sobering. One stormy afternoon in the fall I was walking alone by a stream near our home when the sky darkened and turned green, the air went dead, and there was a chilling silence. Tornadoes were reported in the area, and I suspected I might be in eye of one. But this seemed different. Suddenly I sensed evil surrounding me and I wanted to run. But instead I stood my ground, confessed faith in Christ and his power over all of creation and the evil one. Then, in a still, small voice, the Holy Spirit reminded me that "we do not wrestle against flesh and blood, but against the rulers, against the authorities, against the cosmic powers over this present darkness, against the spiritual forces of evil in heavenly places" (Ephesians 6:12). This experience brought to mind Psalm 23:4, "Even though I walk through the valley of shadow of death, I will fear no evil, for you are with me."

I have never had an experience like that since, but that vision of evil is enough to keep me levelheaded and trusting God in the battle until Christ's return.

Divisions from Within

No school of discipleship is complete without learning how to handle disagreements, divisions, even splits. We arrived in Mansfield starry-eyed, thoroughly committed to living out Acts 4:32, "Now the full number of those who believed were of one heart and soul, and no one said that any of the things that belonged to him was his own, but they had everything in common." We looked out for each other and for the people God brought to our homes.

A new church started at Grace Haven, composed of many people affiliated with the student ministry, including a few students who relocated to be a part of the congregation. Divisions in the church came from two directions: within and without.

As the church grew the elders decided to break it up into seven home churches in neighborhoods around the city. Neighborhood groups, it was hypothesized, were better for outreach, community, and discipleship. In theory, that is correct. To maintain overall unity, leaders from the seven churches met regularly under the leadership of Tim Barber, a man of high character and integrity. Further, the home churches worshipped together in the Grace Haven Lodge once a month. The proposal was sound, but the execution was wanting.

Gifted leaders led the home churches. Unfortunately, three of them strongly disagreed with Tim Barber's leadership. We were disheartened as churches evolved into factions, much like the divisions in the church that the apostle Paul addresses in his first letter to the Corinthians.

Further, hidden character flaws in these leaders—much like coral reefs lying just below the surface of calm waters—were exposed by the ebb and flow of pastoral pressures and temptations.

John Wimber once said, "Gifts and abilities, no matter how magnificent, are either limited or enhanced by character." Tragic stories of broken lives resulted.

Disheartened but not broken, I looked for leadership takeaways. First, gifted leaders who lack character development are dangerous. The biggest problems were created by the most charismatic leaders. Ray Nethery prioritized moral and ethical qualities over gifting and charisma, observing that most discipleship programs neglect character formation.

In his book *The Great Omission: Reclaiming Jesus's Essential Teachings on Discipleship,* Dallas Willard wrote that the most significant factor in the decline of Christianity in the west is "the absence of a coherent teaching and practice of discipleship, and its goal in spiritual formation. It is the scandal of the 'Great Omission of the Great Commission.'" Willard believed kingdom life has begun now, and deep soul transformation is possible, because of our union with Christ. Instead of focusing on making disciples, evangelicals have focused on making decisions for Christ. Dallas called this "Bar Code Christianity." Unfortunately, Grace Fellowship had a few "Bar-Code" leaders.

Second, do not quickly lay hands on people. Appointing leaders before they are mature is toxic for the people, and frequently ruins immature leaders' lives as well. Better to grow slowly with integrity than fall into the modern trap of quick growth and short cuts.

Finally, ministries—especially churches—need clearly articulated vision and values that the core leaders agree with—a process that takes time. Top leadership must be unified in heart and mind. In unity, power is released. Divided leadership produces dysfunctional, weak ministries.

Divisions from Without

Grace Fellowship's divisions were complicated by its affiliation with a new church movement, which became known as the New Covenant Apostolic Order (NCAO), composed of ex Campus Crusade staffers. The leadership core was Ray Nethery, Gordon Walker, Peter Gillquist, Ken Berven, Richard Ballew, Jack Sparks, and Jon Braun, their undisputed leader.

Grace Fellowship sponsored NCAO conferences in Mansfield, usually featuring Jon Braun as the main speaker. By 1975, the NCAO had developed a hierarchical model of church administration and was gravitating toward Eastern Orthodoxy. Over time Jon Braun and other key NCAO leaders began teaching Orthodox theological and ecclesiological concepts, without revealing their source. Because of my church history and historical theological studies, I recognized what they were doing.

Eventually a split ensued between those who wanted to become Eastern Orthodox and those who remained in Reformed theology. Ray Nethery and I stayed true to our evangelical roots; the others eventually joined the Antiochian Orthodox Church.

The split was painful, the central issue for me being the NCAO's insistence on decisions of church leaders overruling individual consciences. This extended even to decisions about members' personal lives. In Matthew 20:25–26, Jesus said to the disciples, "You know that the rulers of the Gentiles lord it over them, and their great ones exercise authority over them. It shall not be so among you." One night I went to sleep an evangelical Christian, and the next morning I woke up being told I should be an Eastern Orthodox believer. This was a proclamation not a process.

I was not happy.

Feeling deeply violated and saddened, I held firm because I knew what I believed—the Gospel, what Christ has done for me—and why I believed it. When I talked to my heart, I had an assurance of salvation that gave me a profound peace and joy. No accusation could shake me; no attack could separate me from God's love.

Eastern Orthodoxy is not heresy; in fact, I grew spiritually through a deeper understanding of Orthodox theology and tradition. My objection was to the profound violation of my conscience, something true Eastern Orthodox theology would never advocate.

The *Westminster Confession of Faith*, Chapter 20, says it well:

> God alone is Lord of the conscience... So that to believe such doctrines, or to obey such commands out of conscience, is to betray true liberty of conscience; and the requiring of an implicit faith, and an absolute and blind obedience, is to destroy liberty of conscience, and reason also.

The division contributed to the local church's struggles, creating greater disunity. Grace Fellowship took another body blow, losing more spiritual vitality. Members lost confidence in the church, a few drifting away and moving to other churches or cities.

This episode of my life was especially painful because Jon Braun meant so much to Suzanne and me. He had inspired me to pursue a high calling, performed our marriage, and participated in my ordination. We loved and appreciated him. But he wanted us to cross a line we could not cross—to put his voice ahead of God's voice. Submission to delegated authority is foundational to spiritual health, but that authority cannot usurp the word of God or ask anyone to go against conscience.

A fundamental principle of hearing Big Words from God is a radical commitment to putting him first in your life. In 2002 I wrote in my journal these words about our time in Mansfield: "I learned a valuable lesson: Ministry is war; you will get wounded, and the most hurtful wounds come from brothers and sisters."

The Seven-Year Itch

In 1976, we resigned as Grace Haven householders. After six extraordinary, challenging, and remarkable years in God's school of discipleship, the Holy Spirit was calling us to a new adventure. We needed family renewal time to think and pray. One era was ending, though we were unsure about our next assignment. So, we moved off the farm into a duplex in town and started asking God for a Big Word.

Initially, we were thinking that perhaps we would move back to California. But to what were we moving? Or should I pursue my PhD in Church History and then return to a professorship at Ashland Theological Seminary? The University of Michigan had an outstanding history program, and after visiting Ann Arbor—we loved the university city—we thought it might be the place for us. Ray reminded us that Ann Arbor was close to several supportive churches in our growing church association, so it made sense to start there. Ray and I also had a relationship with Floyd Robinson, a generous supporter from Flint, Michigan, who offered financial help if we planted a church.

As we prayed, God spoke a Big Word: Ann Arbor is the place. In 1977, we left Mansfield behind, but did not leave our friendships behind. To this day we maintain contact with many close friends from our Buckeye days.

SIX

In the School of Leadership

Ann Arbor & Port Huron, Michigan

"Godly leadership is not about attaining
recognition or glory; it's about serving others.
The big deal is we think the power is in us individually.
The power is in us collectively. It is in the church."
—John Perkins

My older brother, Robin, was a career naval aviator. In the early 1980s, he invited me to join him for a tour of the USS John F. Kennedy, the last conventionally powered carrier built for the US Navy. His rank was Commander, one of ten cabinet officers on the floating city that housed over 4,000 sailors. As we walked through the ship, bow to stern and back, sailors snapped to attention and saluted him.

"Boy," I observed, "My job as a leader would be lot easier if I had stripes on my shoulders like you."

"Kevin," he said, "if you think my rank is the only basis for authority and respect, you don't understand effective leadership. While my rank gives me authority and compels men and women of lower rank to show respect and comply with my commands, something else is needed if they will work under me in a consistent and constructive way. I've learned I must sincerely care for those under me, without giving away any of my authority."

My brother understood the method of the Master. Jesus, the greatest leader and most brilliant and powerful man to walk the earth, taught his disciples at the Last Supper, "Let the greatest among you become as the youngest, and the leader as one who serves... I am among you as one who serves" (Luke 22:26–27). And he modeled servant leadership at the Last Supper when he washed their feet (John 13:1–20). The truth of Christ that we know *and do* sets us apart as leaders. In the kingdom of God, up is down and down is up.

Servant leadership meant cultivating and growing the resources God entrusted to me—preeminently the gospel and my gifts and talents—always for the sake of others. This is an unconditional calling. Jesus loved his disciples "to the end," even when they abandoned him (John 13:1). I had learned much about servant leadership from Ray Nethery, but my response to Robin's observations told me I needed to learn more. Much more.

Learning and living servant leadership was God's agenda for us when he sent us out on our first ministry posting. "In your next phase of ministry," Ray told me before leaving Ohio, "God will be more interested in what he's going to do to you than through you." That was a prophetic Big Word that helped me navigate the twists and turns, the ups and downs, the successes and failures of our tenure in Michigan.

Ann Arbor

Ann Arbor is the most highly educated city in the United States. One hundred nine thousand people lived there in 1977, approximately 40,000 of whom were students at the University of Michigan. Employing more than 25,000 people, the university was the town's economic and intellectual focal point. Ann Arbor was the "Berkeley of the Midwest"—known for radical political activism and a lax attitude toward cannabis.

Mansfield was our school of discipleship; Ann Arbor would become our school of leadership. Suzanne and I were twenty-nine years old when we left Mansfield. For seven years we had done many good things to discover the best. We left with a clear understanding of our strengths and weaknesses, which were learned through experience and were confirmed by Ray and other colleagues. Suzanne's primary gifts were encouragement, hospitality, administration, and teaching, which were seasoned with wisdom and occasional prophetic words.

My primary gifts were teaching (including writing), evangelism, and leadership. I am an influencer and networker. My leadership gifting is catalytic and entrepreneurial: planting new ministries and congregations; identifying and equipping younger leaders; encouraging pastors and shepherds to step out in faith. Administration is not my strength, I quickly lose interest in staff meetings or board meetings, although I endure them to accomplish a greater goal.

Suzanne tempers my risk taking with her level-headed ability to count the cost, which helps avoid impetuous, foolish decisions. She is also a capable administrator, because she pays attention to detail, which is why she is a talented copy editor and gifted financial manager.

Stuart and Peggy Brown, Dave McGlothlin, and Art Casci sensed the Holy Spirit leading them to join us in Ann Arbor. Stuart,

Peggy, and Dave had attended the College of Wooster; Art was a student at Grace Haven. Our vision was to live in community, win the lost, and plant a church. Floyd Robinson helped us buy a large, run-down house on the corner of Miller and Gott in the multi-ethnic Water Hill District, west of downtown Ann Arbor. The house was already divided into three apartments for student housing and desperately needed renovation. A few months after moving in, we added a second story with volunteer builders from a church in Michigan's Upper Peninsula. We lived in a construction zone for a couple of months.

Suzanne in front of our Ann Arbor home, 1978

My plan was to take the Graduate Record Exam (GRE), then matriculate at the University of Michigan PhD history program. After studying for a couple of months in our dingy, damp basement, I took the GRE, did well, and was accepted into graduate school. That part of the plan went well. However, I wasn't convinced I should pursue an academic career.

Unfortunately, the church plant never took off. We found it difficult to connect with people, which surprised me. Two couples and a single—our daughter's elementary school principal, Rhoda Pierre—joined the six of us for Sunday worship, but not much else happened. I was frustrated, wondering why God sent us to Ann Arbor. I asked myself some difficult questions. Was I resorting to counseling God in my prayers? Was I going about things in the wrong way? Was I acknowledging in my heart that his judgments are unsearchable and his ways inscrutable? Was I wrestling with God or trusting in his sovereign character?

Timothy Keller says, "Many times people think if God has called you to something, he's promising you success. He might be calling you to fail to prepare you for something else through the failure." This was one of those times.

The Word of God Community

Authentic assessment of failure or success is based on God's evaluation, not my expectation. He had another purpose for sending us to Ann Arbor. Shortly after moving to town, Suzanne and I attended a musical play at the Power Center Theater on the University of Michigan campus. The Word of God Community, a 1,500-member, ecumenical, charismatic group, was performing a theatrical outreach. Over 1,000 people packed the auditorium.

At intermission I felt a tap on my shoulder. "Who are you?" Bert Ghezzi, one of the community leaders, was sitting directly behind us; he noticed our positive, animated response to the talented and engaging presentation of various biblical parables. We had a short conversation, exchanged telephone numbers, and a few days later Bert invited us to his home to meet his wife Mary Lou and get to know each other. Bert, who had earned a PhD in history from Notre Dame, was the perfect connection. His warm, engaging personality motivated me to learn more about the community; he introduced me to other members.

Founded in 1967, the Word of God Community grew out of the Catholic charismatic renewal. Most community members were Roman Catholic. On Sunday morning the members attended their individual churches, then gathered together in the afternoon. We attended a few of their general assemblies and were impressed by the depth of worship and the presence of the Holy Spirit. The teaching was outstanding. Though not Pentecostals, the community believed in and practiced all the spiritual gifts, and they did it in an orderly, biblical fashion. The sick were prayed for and prophetic words spoken. Suzanne and I felt at home.

Had I decided to matriculate at the University of Michigan, we would have seriously considered becoming members of the Word of God community. But that was not to be. I needed a Big Word from God but heard nothing—neither yes nor no. God's timing is always perfect, never too early, never too late. I could wait.

A marvelous blessing that year was the birth of Alyssa Grace, born at home on June 19, 1978. Our family was complete: Two Buckeyes and one Wolverine. We were young and poor, but confident that God knew our future and it was good.

The Port Huron Declaration

God had called us to Michigan—we did not doubt it—but what was he up to? His purpose was not what we thought it would be. Then a door opened, and we sensed a calling to Port Huron, one hundred miles northeast of Ann Arbor.

About forty believers invited us to start a new church, and as we evaluated our situation it seemed like the prudent move. Stuart and

Peggy Brown also felt called to move with us. The two single men, Dave and Art, were established in Ann Arbor. Art had enrolled in Concordia College, and was considering the Lutheran ministry— he eventually became a Missouri Synod Lutheran pastor. Dave secured a good position at the university.

Port Huron made sense because it was close enough to Ann Arbor to maintain a relationship with the Word of God community and was within commuting distance of the University of Western Ontario in London, Ontario. I had not ruled out earning my PhD in church history. I thought it would be wise to take a couple of graduate history courses to see if academic life was for me. The University of Western Ontario presented the opportunity.

In 1978, Port Huron was a typical upper-Midwest rust-belt town, struggling economically from the shrinking Detroit automobile industry and stagnant population growth. Strategically located at the base of Lake Huron, which emptied into the St. Clair River, Port Huron was an international border crossing point, connecting Michigan to Sarnia, Ontario, via the Blue Water Bridge.

The St. Clair River is a significant section of the Great Lakes Waterway, connecting the Atlantic Ocean to the Great Lakes via the St. Lawrence Seaway. Massive cargo ships from all over the world navigate dangerous currents under the Blue Water Bridge as they head up Lake Huron and down Lake Michigan to Milwaukee and Chicago. Port Huron was also home to a Coast Guard Station; several Coasties would become members of the new church.

During my first year in Port Huron I commuted sixty miles once a week to London, Ontario, to study "Selected Topics in the Age of the Renaissance and Reformation." Building a close relationship with my professor (he even visited our home in Port Huron), his observations helped me discern if an academic career was for me. I enjoyed the research, such as writing papers on *Petrarch's Ascent of Mt. Ventoux* and John Calvin's *Ecclesiastical Ordinances of 1541*. But the idea of developing curricula and course material, conducting research, "publishing or perishing," attending conferences, and participating in endless committee, departmental, and faculty meetings did not appeal to me. Further, my personality is not well suited for the notorious departmental politics common to most colleges and universities. After much prayer, discussion with Suzanne, and contemplation, I decided not to pursue a PhD. That door was finally closed.

Open Hearts, Open Home

The church, named Agape Community, met at the YMCA and grew steadily the first year, soon topping one hundred members. Suzanne and I opened our lives to new people. Looking at a collection of photographs from that era, I'm impressed by our sense of community. We had singles live with us over the years, several of them with great needs. Our dinner table often had guests. Disciples are made by what is taught and what is caught, and that comes in community, generosity, and hospitality.

As a young pastor, I approached ministry with a positive, expectant faith. I believed God was working to transform lives by his grace, and if I sincerely trusted him and stepped out in integrity, people would follow.

I was right about God's transforming power, but very wrong about people's response to my leadership. Port Huron is where I re-learned a valuable lesson from Grace Haven: ministry is war, and you will be wounded, usually the most hurtful wounds coming from brothers and sisters.

Agape Community had some momentum going in a town that was significantly churched (mostly Lutheran and Catholic)—no small feat. So far, so good. What I didn't see coming was what Marshall Shelley calls well-intentioned dragons: "Within the church they are often sincere, well-meaning saints, but they leave ulcers, strained relationships, and hard feelings in their wake. They don't consider themselves difficult people. They don't sit up nights thinking of ways to be nasty…. but for some reason, they undermine the ministry of the church" (*Well-Intended Dragons*, p. 11).

My well-intentioned dragon was what Shelley called the "Fickle Financier: This person uses money to register approval or disapproval of church decisions. Sometimes he protests silently by merely withholding offerings" (pg. 39). "John" (not his real name) was the leader of the core of people, many of whom were well-to-do, who had extended to us the call to pastor in Port Huron. He put together the financial package that made it possible for us to move to Port Huron. He was a key influencer in the church.

One day the treasurer called me and said, "The church is in trouble financially. Almost every key giver has stopped giving. John is encouraging his friends to stop giving. Soon we will not be able to pay our bills." There is an adage among pastors that says, "Frequently we are the last to know." Being the last to know, I was caught off guard. Immediately I called John and asked to meet.

"John," I asked, "Are you encouraging your friends to stop giving to the church."

"Yes."

"Why?"

"Because you need to go." John didn't offer more of an explanation, though later I realized his wife was not comfortable in the church, likely creating some stress at home.

"John," I said, "I'm not going to be able to feed my wife and three children. You are starving us out."

"So? I don't care. You are supposed to leave. Just go." John was in his forties, and I was only thirty years old.

Angry, confused, and depressed, I faced what seemed like an impossible problem. "No good deed goes unpunished," I whined to Suzanne and God. But then I quickly pivoted from self-pity to yielding to Christ. If I wallowed too long in defeat, the congregation would be lost. Hearing God's voice is impossible when self-focused. I had to, in Suzanne's words, get out of bed, take a shower, turn to God, and get to work.

When I turned to God—more patient listening, less cacophonous complaining—God spoke, quietly, giving me a risky plan. I thought, "What do I have to lose? I've lost everything anyway."

I called a congregational gathering to explain the church fracture, without bringing accusations or judgments against anyone. Many members were caught off guard. I think John expected me to resign, but—as I said—I am not a quitter. Instead, I talked openly about the financial crisis, without mentioning my personal needs, and acknowledged that many members—about twenty, all big givers—were voting with their wallets.

Then I looked at John and said, "Well, John, you feel strongly about my leadership, so you are now in charge. Agape Community Church is *your* responsibility."

He shot up from his seat, raised his hands in the air like he was surrendering, and declared he did not want *responsibility* for the church. Immediately he walked out.

I looked at the congregation—which was sitting in stunned silence—took a deep breath, and said, "Committing to a new ministry is like committing to your first girlfriend or boyfriend in junior high school. You don't know much about it, and usually the romance doesn't last too long. Joining a new church with new people and a young pastor can be like that—based more on emotion than thoughtful consideration and prayer. So, I propose that each of you take a month off from church to pray and evaluate if Agape Community is for you. Then we will push the re-start button and meet in a month in this room. If you sense you should not continue here, no hard feelings. We will still be friends. If you do show up in four weeks, then Agape Community will move forward."

The congregation needed graciousness, patience, honesty, and love. I had no idea if anyone would come back. About 85 percent of the people returned a month later, and the congregation moved forward. I had passed my first leadership test.

John was never seen again at Agape Community.

The Richest People in the World

Agape Community might not have lost too many members, but the lost members were generous givers. Our budget was crippled, and I had no idea how our family would make it financially. For a second time, God had called me to a town I didn't really want to live in, pulled the financial rug out from under me, and then said, "Learn to serve. Love the people." That was a Big Word, one that can only be responded to with faith. God had me where he wanted me; only his grace and provision could get me through.

I have rarely been motivated by the desire for material comfort or pleasure, so though we were backed into a financial corner, my trust in God never flagged; if anything, I was excited about what he would do next.

In August, we flew home to California for a vacation. I was anxious about our financial situation. A few years ago, our oldest daughter Kelley wrote a paper for graduate school in which she reflected on her upbringing with these words: "As a child [in Ann

Arbor] we lived in a low-income neighborhood. *Indeed, my family was poor*, although at the time I did not know that we were in the lower economic strata."

While in California we visited Alberta Keeby. Alberta worked for Suzanne's parents—living with the family—while Suzanne was growing up. Being raised in an African American church in the south and with only a third-grade education, Alberta had a profound spiritual influence on Suzanne and her entire family. She was a special person, strategically placed by God in the Nadal family as a witness for Christ.

When Suzanne's father retired, they moved to Fallbrook, an avocado growing town in northern San Diego County. They asked Alberta to move with them, but she said no, because she wanted to stay close to her adult daughter in nearby Wilmington. Fortunately, the new owners of their Rolling Hills home—the Higholts—retained her. We visited Alberta twice in Suzanne's old Possum Ridge Road home.

Rolling Hills is a private, gated city, offering high security for its residents. Carlisle Wrigley Higholt was the mother of a four-year old son, Jonathan. Carlisle was also a Wrigley chewing gum heiress, the great-granddaughter of William Wrigley, Jr., owner of the Chicago Cubs, the Wrigley gum company, and Catalina Island. Having met Carlisle two years earlier, we knew she was emotionally fragile, living in fear because of anonymous death threats and actual violent crimes against Wrigley heirs. Four years earlier, a Wrigley relative was murdered and packed in wet cement in Los Angeles. Another son, Marc Wrigley, had died at age two from a heart ailment. Carlisle was forty years old but looked like she was sixty; she was a tortured soul.

When Suzanne and I and our three children met with Alberta, Carlisle joined the conversation. She described her profound despair, and we shared with her about the peace of Christ. Carlisle told us she had met and prayed with Cardinal John Cody, Archbishop of Chicago, and with Billy Graham, but God's peace eluded her. In a private moment, Alberta told us Carlisle slept on a spare bed in her room almost every night.

When we left, Carlisle walked out to the car with us and said, "You are the richest people I have ever met." We did not have two nickels to rub together, but we were the richest people she knew. My perspective on material wealth was changed that day. That was a Big Word from God. A truth which I had known in my head—the "Father of our Lord Jesus Christ... has blessed us in Christ with every spiritual blessing in the heavenly places" (Ephesians 1:3)—penetrated my heart.

When I am stressed about our personal finances, I think of Carlisle Wrigley Higholt's words—"You are the richest people I have ever met"—and thank God that we are indeed rich in Christ. Jesus says, "Seek first the kingdom of God and his righteousness, and all these things will be added to you" (Matthew 6:33). The truth of prosperity and peace is simple: Put God first, and he will give you exactly what you need—not necessarily what you want, but always what you need. That's the secret to contentment, in plenty and in want.

That night we flew home to Detroit. On the drive to Port Huron from the airport, I turned on a local radio station and heard a news flash: "Carlisle Wrigley Higholt, the Wrigley gum heiress, is dead from a tragic stabbing." Later we learned it was self-inflicted.

Servant Publications

Shortly after returning from California, Servant Publications in Ann Arbor contacted me, asking if I were willing to interview for an editorial position at *Pastoral Renewal* journal. Servant Publications was started by the Word of God Community, and Bert Ghezzi recommended me as a Protestant editor on a majority Catholic staff. *Pastoral Renewal's* 42,000 readers were mostly Catholic priests and evangelical pastors.

In addition to the journal, there was the Center for Pastoral Renewal, which conducted leadership development seminars across North America. This was a significant writing and leadership maturing opportunity, working with writers and speakers like Elisabeth Elliot, Robert Coleman, Donald McGavran, Ted Engstrom, Michael Green, Os Guinness, David Watson, J. I. Packer, Paul Vitz, Dallas Willard, C. Peter Wagner, Ralph Martin, Sister Ann Shields, and Peter Williamson.

Our move to Michigan had led to post-graduate enrollment in God's school of leadership. Reflecting on these events, I see God's providence, which J. Vernon McGee defines as:

> . . . *the means by which God directs all things—both animate and inanimate, seen and unseen, good and evil—toward a worthy purpose, which means His will must finally prevail . . . Our God is running the universe today, even though there are some who think that it has slipped out from under Him. Providence is the way that God is directing the universe. He is moving it into tomorrow—He is moving it into the future by His providence. Providence means "to provide." God will provide.*

Needing to live in Port Huron to pastor Agape Community, I could only work half-time. Servant agreed to my conditions, even offering a room with a family for my weekly two-days in the office. I also worked in my home office. Our financial needs were met. God provided, and we felt like the richest people in the world.

My responsibilities at *Pastoral Renewal* were roughly divided between writing and editing articles for the journal and coordinating special projects like leaders' conferences. Kevin Perrotta oversaw my writing, which I quickly learned was wanting. I will never forget his editing marks on my first assignment. The pages were a sea of red. Kevin is an outstanding writer and editor. He is also one of the most brilliant people I have ever known. I admire him greatly. So, I decided: My goal is to be able to write just like Kevin Perrotta.

I rewrote the first article, and it came back with fewer editorial markings. I rewrote it again. And again. And again. When I decided to become a writer, no one told me that most of what I wrote would be tripe. No one tells you that the "only kind of writing is," in the words of Ernest Hemmingway, "rewriting." Getting something right the first time is as rare as hitting an inside-the-park home run. I should have known that. In my USC days I had taken a creative writing course and the professor's only comment on my feeble attempt at writing fiction was, "This is crap." (To be honest, it was unreadable.)

But I persevered, and Kevin persevered with me. Each assignment improved a little, if only 1 percent, but movement was in the right direction. Then a breakthrough came about a year-and-a-half into my Servant Publications tenure. Ann Spangler, the editor of *New Covenant* magazine, a Catholic publication, asked me to write an article. I cannot remember the topic, but she loved the result. "Well, Ann," I told her, "I try to write just like Kevin Perrotta."

"But Kevin," she said, "You don't write like Kevin Perrotta at all. Your personality is different from his; your personality comes through in your writing. Your writing is unique to you and is authentic."

Men and women have said to me, "If I give myself completely to Christ, I will lose my individuality, my uniqueness. That's asking too much." It is true that when someone prays, "I'm giving my entire life to you God," he says, "I'll take it. All of it." But when God takes your life, he reforms and transforms your soul, returning it to you newer, cleaner, clearer, and brighter in every way. God is not in the personality *obliteration* business; he is in the personality *regeneration* business. "Men [and women] are never so truly and fully personal," Charles Hummel wrote in *The Tyranny of the Urgent*, "as when they are living in complete dependence upon God."

The gospel writers Matthew, Mark, and John were committed to becoming just like their Master. They were passionately devoted to their Rabbi, noting everything he said and did. They listened, watched, imitated, and obeyed him to become like him. Discipleship was an intense, intentional, personal system of education. Every sphere of their life was conformed to Christ's character—body, soul, mind, spirit, emotions, economics, sexuality, relationships—everything. Did they lose their individuality? Hardly. Read the New Testament Gospels: each unique in style, God's truth filtered through three distinctive temperaments.

That same principle was at work when I was Kevin Perrotta's writing apprentice. Kevin P is analytical, reflective, and insightful. He's a Catholic with a rich prayer and Scripture study life. Kevin S, on the other hand, is an activist who frequently talks before he thinks. I am a Protestant creative leader. One an introvert; the other an extrovert. God's truth filters through two distinct personalities. When we write, our personalities express themselves automatically and unconsciously.

There was more to our relationship than work. Kevin and Mary Perrotta and their six children hosted me in their home when I stayed in Ann Arbor. We became close, our families becoming life-long friends. During this time Mary became ill with cancer. There was a lot of prayer, love, and bonding.

Mary Kathleen Perrotta went to be with the Lord in paradise on April 15, 1989.

Mahesh Chavda

My Michigan years were challenging on three levels. First, my family: Suzanne and I now had three children; we were no longer young marrieds. Our children were growing up quickly, involved in church, school, and athletics. This was fun but a busy time. Suzanne and I worked hard at communication and trust, and our marriage held up well during this era.

Second, as Agape Community Church grew, ministry became more complicated and time consuming. John Wimber once said, "Pastors are in the people processing business, and people take time." Because I worked half-time at Servant Publications, delegation was the key to building a healthy congregation. I was good but not great at delegating. Add to that the pressure of preaching almost every week, and I often fell short.

Third, my professional life at Servant: Learning to write, interacting with key national leaders, travel, and coordinating leadership conferences were challenging events but highly fulfilling. However, I had too much on my plate.

My spiritual life began to suffer. I was not devoting the time to disciplines like prayer and worship, meditation and scripture reading. When I turned a deaf ear to God, I listened to other voices—so-called church experts, the hottest spiritual trends, and church growth models. Feeling the pressure to succeed—a drive embedded in me from my upbringing and competitive baseball—I fell into the trap of confusing my calling from God with the demands of people. Allowing their expectations to shape my ministry was a prescription for failure. I was beginning to question my calling to the Port Huron church, feeling I had completed my part in planting the church and it was time for us to move on. I was suffering a holy discontent.

By 1983, I was burnt out, badly in need of spiritual renewal. That's when Bert Ghezzi suggested I attend a Mahesh Chavda seminar in East Lansing at Michigan State University. Mahesh, raised a devout Hindu in India, became disenchanted at age thirteen and converted to Christ at age sixteen after reading the Gospel of John. Coming from the princely Rajput caste, Mahesh was the first known member of his family in eight hundred years to become a Christian. I cannot remember the topic of the evening, but when Mahesh finished speaking, he invited anyone in the crowd of approximately 150 to receive prayer. Mahesh, Bert told me, had a powerful prayer ministry, especially when praying for people to be renewed by the Holy Spirit.

Desperate, I walked forward to receive prayer. As Mahesh and I chatted about our mutual friend Bert and Servant Publications, I became aware of a force field—I don't know any other way to describe it—scanning my body as we talked, accentuated by his hand gestures. He was not praying, but I could feel waves of God's power in my body. Then he asked, "How can I pray for you?"

"I'm burnt out, tired, in need of God's recharging power in my life."

"Sure." Without touching me, Mahesh prayed, "Okay, Holy Spirit come and renew brother Kevin." Remarkably simple; very direct. And then—*bam!*—the Holy Spirit threw me backwards in the air ten feet against a wall, and I crumpled to the floor.

I was not hurt, and I was not knocked unconscious. Quite the contrary, I was intensely conscious, and aware of the refreshing infilling of the Holy Spirit. The renewing presence of God awakened me several times that night, the Holy Spirit moving through my body.

Jesus delivered me from my malaise. My mind was focused, prayer and scripture reading energized, and my preaching elevated. God was preparing me for my next stage of ministry.

A Third Wave

Shortly after this experience, Kevin Perrotta and I interviewed C. Peter Wagner for the *Pastoral Renewal* journal. Dr. Wagner was a professor of church growth at Fuller Theological Seminary's School of World Missions in Pasadena, California. He was a key leader of the church growth movement. During the interview he described a "third wave of the Holy Spirit"—following Pentecostalism (the "first wave") and the charismatic movement (the "second wave")— that was renewing conservative evangelical Protestants. The interview, titled "A Third Wave?" was published in the July–August 1983 *Pastoral Renewal*.

Dr. Wagner encouraged us to contact his friend John Wimber, the senior pastor of the Anaheim Vineyard Christian Fellowship who, along with him, was teaching a course at Fuller Seminary titled "MC 510: Signs, Wonders, and Church Growth." I decided to interview John and published it in *Commonlife* magazine. The interview changed my life.

John called me shortly after reading the article. "You are the first journalist to understand what I'm saying and doing, and you write it better than I can. We have to meet." After a long discussion, I asked if he would pray for me over the phone. Bam! It happened again. The Holy Spirit knocked me off my chair and God's power went through me. That night I was awakened again as the Holy Spirit swept through my body. Speaking at a men's conference in Toledo, Ohio, the following weekend, as I gestured my hand to make a point, a wave of the Holy Spirit's power hit a row of men and knocked them off their seats. I was as astonished as they were.

A few days later I received another call from John. "Can you fly down to Houston next weekend? I'm speaking at a conference there and I'd like to meet with you in person. I'll pay for your ticket."

"Sure." We met in Houston between his speaking sessions. That was the beginning of a partnership and friendship that would last until his death.

A few days after I returned home from Houston, John phoned again, telling me that for three years he had been sitting on book contracts, waiting for God to show him who should be his writing partner. John was a powerful leader, persuasive speaker, and gifted musician, but he had neither the time nor background to write books. Then he said, "You are the one Carol and I have been praying for, for three years. Would you pray about signing contracts with Hodder & Stoughton in Great Britain, and Harper & Row Publishers in the United States?" These were two of the most prestigious English language publishers in the world.

This was a Big Word, a life-changing word from God.

I flew to California, met with John to hammer out details— book topics, contract terms, and how our writing relationship would work. We signed contracts for four books. John decided the topic of our first book would be evangelism, the second healing. Eventually they were titled *Power Evangelism* and *Power Healing*.

A Long Goodbye

One condition of signing with John was that we move to Orange County, California. In addition to writing the books, John planned on my editing *Equipping the Saints* magazine, assisting him as he wrote conference lectures and sermons, and other assignments.

I was overwhelmed by a feeling of inadequacy. Here's how I prayed: "Write books? I hardly know where to start! I am no Kevin Perrotta or Ann Spangler. What have I gotten myself into? This is out of my league." To use a baseball analogy, one day I was languishing on the minor league Toledo Mud Hens, the next I was called up to hit cleanup for the Los Angeles Dodgers.

Then God reminded me of Jeremiah, Paul, and Moses.

When God called Jeremiah to be a prophet to the nations, Jeremiah said, "Ah, Lord God! Behold, I do not know how to speak, for I am only a youth." God responded, "Do not say, 'I am only a youth'; for to all to whom I send you, you shall go . . . for I am with you to deliver you" (Jeremiah 1:6–8). When God calls, he always equips. Unknown to me, the work I was called to do would go to the nations! Our books would be translated into many languages and John would speak all over the world. I am no Jeremiah, but I identify with his insecurities.

When the Apostle Paul felt inadequate, God said, "My grace is sufficient for you, for my power is made perfect in weakness." Paul concluded, "For when I am weak, then I am strong" (2 Corinthians 12:9, 10). My weakness was the fear of falling flat on my face, of failing God and John Wimber. "Okay, Lord," I prayed, "once again you've got me where you want me. I'll find my strength in you."

I identified with both Jeremiah and Paul! "I'm up to bat with the bases loaded facing Sandy Koufax's curve ball. Help!" God answered, "Take it one pitch at a time."

But I still needed help.

Then Moses at the burning bush came to mind. When God spoke a Big Word to him, Moses said, "Oh, my Lord, I am not eloquent... I am slow of speech and of tongue." God responded, "Who has made man's mouth? . . . Is it not I, the Lord? Now therefore go, and I will be with your mouth and teach you what you shall speak" (Exodus 4:10–12).

"But Lord," Moses said, "I can't do it!"

"Okay," the Lord responded, "your brother Aaron will help you." God promised Moses that he would teach him how to speak, and when Moses asked God for more help, he was given Aaron.

And more help is what God provided for me.

God said, "Go. Take this new assignment." But then he said, "Wait." Let me explain. By go, he meant start writing the book now; by wait, he said, stay another year in Michigan. Suzanne prayed and sensed God wanted us to stay one more year so we could leave Agape Community Church with integrity. Because we make big decisions together, I waited for Suzanne to feel peace and release from the Lord to move. I was not happy. I wanted to turn to the next chapter of my life. Frequently God clarifies his will for me through my wife's prayers and insights.

As it turned out, by staying that extra year, God gave me the extra help that I had prayed for. I remained at Servant Publications, where Kevin Perrotta, once again, coached and encouraged me in writing John's and my first book. God gave him, and John Blattner—another editor who had written several books—to me.

Our last year in Michigan was bitter-sweet. When God called Suzanne and me to open our hearts and home in Port Huron, we learned that serving was the key to forming lasting relationships. But now God was calling us away from brothers and sisters like Stuart and Peggy Brown, Larry and Kris Smith, Gary and Sue Schroyer, Bruce and Judy Kirkpatrick, Bob McPherson, Roger and

Ellen Thomas, and many others. Leaving was difficult, but when God changes your life with a Big Word, you must step out in faith.

In early December of 1984, we loaded our car and a small U-Haul truck and traversed the interstate highways to California. We pushed through snowstorms, lost control on icy roads, almost flipped the U-Haul under the St. Louis Gateway Arch, and drove through gusty southwestern deserts to our new home. We were, in the words of Al Jolson (written by Bud De Sylva and Joseph Meyer), in "California Here I Come," coming right back to where we started from.

When the wintry winds are blowing and the snow is starting in to fall,
then my eyes turn west-ward, knowing that's the place I love the best of all.
California, I've been blue, since I've been away from you.
I can't wait 'til I get going.
Even now I'm starting in to call, Oh . . .
California, here I come right back where I started from.

Home again!

SEVEN

The Wimber Years

Yorba Linda, California

"The authority by which the Christian leader leads is not power but love, not force but example, not coercion but reasoned persuasion. Leaders have power, but power is safe only in the hands of those who humble themselves to serve."
—John Stott, *Issues Facing Christians Today*

Before moving to California, I received a Big Word that would anchor me for the next ten years of my life. As I prayed about my relationship with John Wimber, God said, "You are to serve John faithfully until he retires or dies. Submit to him, protect him, remain loyal to him." That word was unusually clear. Evidently my next assignment would have more to it than ghost writing books. Oswald Chambers observed in *My Utmost for His Highest*:

Readiness for God means that we are prepared to do the smallest thing or the largest thing—it makes no difference. It means we have no choice in what we want to do, but that whatever God's plans may be, we are there and ready. Whenever any duty presents itself, we hear God's voice as our Lord heard His Father's voice, and we are ready for it with the total readiness of our love for Him.

I was ready for God, so when he said serve and submit, protect and remain loyal, to the best of my ability, I was ready to obey.

Big Words are of no value unless followed from the heart; they are not big suggestions. In the Old Testament, King Saul received a Big Word when Samuel told him to wait seven days for him in Gilgal before sacrificing peace offerings and going to war against the powerful Philistines (1 Samuel 13:8). Earlier Samuel had instructed Saul to "Fear the Lord and serve him faithfully *with all your heart*" (1 Samuel 12:24). But Saul became impatient and fearful when Samuel was delayed. His warriors were abandoning him, so Saul panicked and disobeyed God's Big Word. Saul failed a significant test: he did not obey God from his heart. Fearing man more than God, disobedience cost him everything—his family, his kingship, and eventually his life.

Richard Foster, in *The Celebration of Discipline*, wrote, "Submission is the ability to lay down the terrible burden of always needing to get our own way." That was my experience; this is freedom in Christ. The next ten years were the most joyful, fruitful, and fulfilling times of my life.

But I'm getting ahead of the story.

Culture Shock

Moving to California meant leaving intentional Christian community behind. For fifteen of the first sixteen years of our marriage we opened our homes to single Christians, married couples, and families. When we lived in Ohio, a neighbor's home burned down, and we invited Chet and Carol Weigle and their four young children to move in with us for several months while they rebuilt. Our supper table regularly had guests, and we never suffered a shortage of food or babysitters. Family life was chaotic at times but always authentic and never boring. They were happy, exhausting days.

However, Suzanne and I decided when we moved back to California to pull back on Christian community to focus on family. Our children were growing up and needed more, not less, of our attention. We also wanted to create more space in our lives to reconnect with our parents and siblings.

Although not conscious of it at the time, the transition to a megachurch culture—more individualistic and fast-paced—was stressful. The Anaheim Vineyard Christian Fellowship's attendance fluctuated between four- and five-thousand, and John Wimber regularly hosted international leaders' conferences that ran in the thousands.

What You See Is What You Get

My first day on the job in Anaheim, John Wimber said to me, "You are going to cause ripples." I was not surprised. John had recruited me for more than my writing ability. He felt my background in community, disciple making, and interdenominational parachurch work provided perspective that was lacking in the nascent Vineyard movement. My California roots did not hurt either.

Many of John's young leaders were homegrown; in most cases they had at best nominal church upbringings. I observed this when, a few months before moving to Yorba Linda, John invited the Center for Pastoral Renewal to conduct a leaders' training seminar in Anaheim. Peter Williamson, Dave Nodar and I taught twenty-five young leaders-in-training for two days on the topics of leadership and character formation. Apart from Ken Fish, every participant turned a deaf ear to our words. Through body language and tone, they communicated the conference was beneath them. We had conducted these events across North America to many high-level pastoral leaders far more mature and accomplished than these interns, and never encountered this kind of resistance.

John Wimber was not surprised. He was a man of integrity, and he wanted to raise up young leaders with the inner strength to withstand the outward pressures of the ministry. Uncorrected youthful character flaws become significant liabilities as leaders age and take on positions of authority.

John was more concerned about character growth than he was about charismatic gifts. When people asked me, "What was John really like?" I would say, "What you see is what you get. Like all the disciples in scripture, he isn't perfect. But he is humble, honest, generous, and has a soft heart."

My Boss, My Friend

John was more than my boss; he also became a friend. It was not unusual for us to eat lunch together two or three times a week, and occasionally go out to dinner with our wives. I usually met John in his Yorba Linda home, reviewing book material, sermons, and conference talks. My commitment was to protect John, editing his work to avoid any misunderstandings or misrepresentations. I accomplished this by asking questions that would spur him to clarify his thoughts. All this work was *his* work; my job was to facilitate the delivery. We worked well together. He trusted me from the beginning, which was humbling.

As our relationship developed, our conversations segued to challenging pastoral situations and complicated leadership relationships. I would listen, and over time he asked for my observations. John quickly placed a governor on our relationship when, in the middle of a conversation in which I offered my opinion, he interrupted me. "Kevin, you just used three words that I don't ever want to hear from you in our relationship: *You Have To*." That was a good reminder that God called me to serve, submit, protect, and remain loyal to him.

John's task was daunting, ministering to top leaders from many traditions: Presbyterians, Baptists, Roman Catholics, Lutherans, Pentecostals, Methodists, Episcopalians, and many others. These leaders came from all over the world. Because I was raised in the Episcopal Church but served in evangelical and Catholic interdenominational parachurch ministries, I understood many of the ecclesiological, theological, and cultural differences. John occasionally asked me to represent him at meetings with national leaders from a variety of ministries when he was too busy to attend.

Further, John oversaw what I call a three-ring circus. First, there was Vineyard Ministries International (VMI), a parachurch ministry that took him around the world speaking to and training thousands of leaders. I was a VMI employee for most of my time in Anaheim. Second was the Vineyard Music Group, a music publishing company that in the 1980s had profound impact on worship music worldwide. Finally, there was the Anaheim Vineyard Christian Fellowship, a mega-church that was part of a loose association of churches started by Kenn Gulliksen. Kenn had founded the first Vineyard Church, which was affiliated with Calvary Chapel; John founded the Vineyard church movement.

Challenges in each arena were daunting. Musicians were frequently upset, pastors were pressuring to start a denomination, the local church had the typical problems with which all local churches struggle. John used to say, "An empty barn is a clean barn. Our barn isn't empty." When John talked with me about these challenges, he wasn't looking for answers, just a person he could trust, a sounding board. Because I spent so much time with him working on publications, frequently I was that person.

With John Wimber, a true and loyal friend

Unnecessary Ripples

Unfortunately, I created a few unnecessary ripples. Shortly after joining the VMI staff, the executive pastor of the Anaheim Vineyard Christian Fellowship called a joint meeting of church and VMI leadership. I only remember one business item from the meeting. An assistant pastor's wife announced that a prominent church member—a single woman—had undergone successful artificial insemination and was due in a few months. She was leaving southern California to have the baby. The pastor and his wife asked that we counter nasty rumors about her.

But something smelled wrong to me, like I was attending a group therapy session in the movie *One Flew Over the Cuckoo's Nest*. The more they talked, the stranger their story sounded. Not thinking—and this is not one of my prouder moments in life—I blurted out, "Where did the insemination take place? In the back seat of a '57 Chevy?" I thought it was a clever remark, but it was not well received, especially by the women. I was banished from church staff meetings after that, not that it bothered me. Ripples indeed.

Sadly, a few weeks later, the pastor's wife who led the discussion was rifling through her husband's desk (did she suspect something?) and found a compromising picture of him with the pregnant single woman. The cat was out of the bag. He resigned from staff, but thankfully the marriage survived.

When I confessed to John my '57 Chevy story, he wasn't surprised. He knew he had unresolved issues on the church staff, many revolving around husband-wife relationships.

We also chatted about our personal lives—family and friends; loyalties and betrayals; triumphs and defeats. These are the things that shape our lives, for better or worse. Our discussions went deep into the stories behind the stories—the kind of things that friends who trust each other talk about. Once in public he shared about his father, saying, "The day I was born, my father took one look at me and left." The crowd laughed, thinking he was joking. I asked him about his dad later, and he said, "He left the day I was born. The next time I saw him I was in my twenties, and his first words to me were, 'Can you hold your liquor like your old man?'" The pain was palpable.

In his classic book, *The Four Loves*, C. S. Lewis observed:

In friendship . . . we think we have chosen our peers . . . But, for a Christian, there are, strictly speaking, no chances. A secret master of

ceremonies has been at work. Christ, who said to the disciples, "You
have not chosen me, but I have chosen you," can truly say to every
group of Christian friends, "You have not chosen one another but I
have chosen you for one another."

A 1983 interview with C. Peter Wagner led to an interview with John Wimber, which led to moving 2,327 miles across the country and finding a new friend. The "secret master of ceremonies" was working, as he does for all of us, creating a new relationship to advance his kingdom.

"You Have to Leave Now"

During my years in Yorba Linda, I was John Wimber's trusted friend, but never accepted in the inner ring of the Vineyard family. I was adopted late into the Vineyard movement, lacking the DNA of home-grown leaders. In fact, my close relationship with John, for whatever reason, created a barrier between me and a few Vineyard pastors. When leaders approached me about opening doors to John, I told them I could not and would not broker my relationship with him. They did not respond well. John liked it that way. He knew my perspective would always be from the outside looking in, which perhaps was more objective. This also aided writing his books and articles.

I remember attending a key national Vineyard leaders' meeting at the Forest Home retreat center in the San Bernardino mountains. John and I talked for hours the week before the gathering; I even came up to Forest Home and roomed next to John and Carol at his invitation. But just prior to the meeting, John said, "Kevin, you have to leave now." I understood. After each session, he processed what transpired with me.

Another time John faced a complicated but potentially unethical pastoral situation involving one of his key national leaders. We discussed the issues extensively before the leader flew in from another part of the country. Just prior to the meeting, John violated his own rule, asking me to participate. As the discussion progressed, John requested that I share my perspective. I was uncomfortable, but not as uncomfortable as the leader. I watched his temperature rise as I laid out our concerns. We agreed to follow up the next morning. Later that night I received a call from John. "Pastor X is incensed that you were included in our meeting. Kevin, you articulated my position well, but it would be best if you were not there tomorrow morning." I was relieved. That leader never talked to me again, even when I reached out to him. God called me to serve John and protect him; by acting as a heat shield, I did that.

The Jazz Artist Theologian

I have been asked which theologians, philosophers, and leaders most influenced John's thinking. C. Peter Wagner, Peter Drucker, and George Eldon Ladd are perhaps at the top of the list. There were other voices from John's years as founding director of the department of church growth at the Charles E. Fuller Institute of Evangelism and Church Growth from 1974 to 1978. By the time we teamed up to write books, he had built a solid Reformed theological base. Theologian Wayne Grudem, a prolific author, had an influence on John's thinking. And there was Gunner Payne, who led John to Christ in 1963, and Lonnie Frisbee, who had a profound impact on John's thinking about the church and the Holy Spirit.

However, what stood out for me in my observation of John was his intuitive and creative leadership. He read people and situations quickly and his analyses were almost always spot on. I believe this had little to do with the theologians and philosophers he read and everything to do with his background as a jazz musician. John spent much of his childhood playing the wind instruments, especially clarinet, saxophone, and trumpet—and almost any other instrument he could get his hands on. He was disciplined and focused, and he brought these traits to his relationship with Christ. He once said to me, "Kevin, as a kid you spent hours outdoors playing sandlot baseball; I was home alone playing my trumpet."

John's wife, Carol, also reminded me that he was a gifted composer and arranger who adapted musical compositions for performance. Ministry was like making music for John, combining a wide variety of people and activities in a way that made the whole bigger than the sum of the parts. Gatherings at conferences and churches usually ended with hundreds of people praying for others, committing their lives to Christ, and walking away determined to take big risks for God. His congregations were his orchestras.

Because jazz musicians work with a wide variety of people—judging them only on their performance, not on race, gender, culture, or education—John saw and called out gifts and strengths in people. He did not have a prejudiced bone in his body, treating everyone alike. This is one reason why believers from a wide variety of Christian traditions, cultures, and ethnicities responded to his ministry. They never felt judged or used by him. Instead, they were affirmed, challenged, and encouraged to do great things for God.

Leaving his music career behind came at a big personal cost. In 1962 and '63 John was a pianist and singer with the Paramours, later known as the Righteous Brothers. In their early years Johnny (as he was called) was the Righteous Brothers manager and he remained their lifelong friend. After John turned to Christ at age twenty-nine, he walked away from the Righteous Brothers shortly after their first hit, "You've Lost That Lovin' Feelin'." Bill Medley and Bobby Hatfield pleaded with him to come back to the group; they recognized and needed his leadership gift. At the time, John was flat broke. But for him there could be no turning back. He had a Big Word: God was calling him to the ministry; it was a higher calling than the legendary Righteous Brothers. No amount of money or fame could deter him.

(Years later Carl Hatfield, Bobby's brother, along with his wife, Jeanne, became members of a church I pastored in Palm Desert. When Carl passed away from Alzheimer's disease on January 9, 2003, I performed his memorial service. Bobby sat in the front row, weeping from grief at the loss of his older brother.)

Possibly John Wimber's natural sensitivities, personality, and gifts—honed through years as a jazz musician, composer, arranger—made him uniquely responsive to the leading of the Holy Spirit. He was remarkably intelligent, living outside the restraints of many Christian organizations that have become rigid boxes, though not outside of orthodox biblical belief. John was an artist-theologian; God used his personality to change the church's experience of prayer, evangelism, and worship music. For his generation he was a significant change agent.

John Wimber was a disrupter. For example, his course MC:510 Signs and Wonders and Church Growth (co-taught with C. Peter Wagner) evoked push back from professors at Fuller Seminary. John was the primary instructor, writing the course outline and teachings. Clinics, where students prayed for the sick, were an integral part of the course. Started in 1982, MC:510 quickly became the most popular and controversial class at Fuller. As a result, a task force of ten faculty members met to evaluate and respond to theological concerns, especially the clinics. (One theology professor was quoted as saying, "We can't pray for the sick here. This is a seminary!")

Shortly after moving to Yorba Linda, I accompanied John to the seminary where he was scheduled to teach a session of MC:510. Before the class began, President David Hubbard's secretary approached John, dismissing him from the course and the seminary. As we drove home, John was as upset as I have ever seen him—not only because he was fired, but because of *how* he was fired. He confided to me in the car that day, "Almost every significant male authority figure in my life has failed me."

The Books

Our first book, *Power Evangelism*, was published in Great Britain on October 1, 1985. The US edition was released May 1, 1986. At that time, the editorial and publishing protocols in the US were more stringent than in the UK, which created delays. The book was quickly published in other languages—German, Dutch, Italian, French, Korean, and Japanese, to name a few.

Much of the writing of *Power Evangelism* took place in Michigan before I moved to California. As soon as I arrived in Yorba Linda, John and I jumped into finalizing the manuscript. My calling was to communicate John's perspectives on how the work of the Holy Spirit impacts evangelism in a way that a wide variety of Christians could understand—not an easy task. We worked from notes and transcriptions developed for his MC:510 Signs and Wonders and Church Growth course, and the less academic conference notes. Jack Sims, Winn Griffin, and Ken Fish had worked with John on these outlines. We met for hours several times a week. I'd go back to my home office, make changes, and then we'd meet again. John diligently labored at clarifying and expanding his teaching. The result was a book that has stood the test of time. In 2006, *Christianity Today* magazine named it the twelfth most significant Christian book published in the preceding fifty years. *Power Evangelism* remains in print today.

I vividly remember the day the Harper & Row edition of *Power Evangelism* arrived at our home. I was excited. Our first book. My name was on the cover. This was one of the biggest days of my life, or so I thought. I could hardly wait to show the book at family dinner that night. "Here it is, kids! The book is out!" They all smiled as I passed it around the room. It took all of one minute for everyone to touch it and say, "Way to go, Dad." Then it was tossed aside on a couch near the dinner table, and an animated discussion about school ensued.

I laughed at myself. I had fallen into the trap of finding my identity in accomplishment, not in Christ. For a moment I had forgotten that my value is rooted in my union with Christ, not in what I do for him. That is the message of the gospel. Fortunately, my children were there to remind me that they love me as a dad, not a writer or leader or speaker or anything else, and Christ loves me as an adopted son and brother.

Power Healing and the *Power Healing Study Guide* were published in 1987. John's intuitive and creative gifting helped him see healing ministry in an evangelical, non-Pentecostal way. At that time, most Christian healing ministries centered on a single man or woman with a powerful healing gift. Sick people attended large gatherings, hoping to receive prayer or touch from a charismatic leader. John saw healing in the Bible operating differently. Jesus modeled healing and trained his disciples how to pray for healing—and then he sent them out to minister in pairs. John loved to say, "Everyone gets to play." He meant all believers can pray for the sick and see positive results. His healing conferences were *equipping* events, teaching the attendees how to pray for members of their families, their friends, their neighbors, anyone.

God used John to influence churches all over the world to develop healing teams who prayed for the sick and trained others to pray for the sick. *Power Healing* addressed biblical and theological issues surrounding divine healing as well as practical teaching on how to pray for the sick. Of the books we wrote together, this is my favorite. It too remains in print today.

In 1988, we wrote *Power Encounters*, a collection of international leaders' testimonies about the work of the Holy Spirit in their lives. (It was titled *Riding the Third Wave* in England.) The book was well received.

In 1991, the third of our "Power Series" with Harper & Row and Hodder & Stoughton was published, titled *Power Points*. This book is different from the first two, emphasizing foundational biblical truths for basic discipleship. John was aware that many evangelicals did not know what they believed nor why they believed it, and he wanted to do something about that. Unfortunately, it did not sell well. It lacked the power-appeal of the first two books. In 1993, John and I collaborated on *The Way to Maturity*, published by Regal Books. *The Way to Maturity* was a small-group study guide and discipleship tool that relied on readings from *Power Points*. Along the way, there was a series of booklets released by Servant Publications.

More Responsibility

Shortly after arriving in Yorba Linda, John asked me to oversee *Equipping the Saints* magazine. With a circulation exceeding 100,000, *Equipping the Saints,* published by Vineyard Ministries

International, targeted leaders in North America, Europe, and Down Under. John wanted to upgrade the magazine's look and content. Magazines were in my wheelhouse, so I quickly instituted much-needed changes, including new and gifted writers from inside and outside the Vineyard stream. I also worked with John on his teaching notes and, with Suzanne, started traveling with Vineyard support teams to major conferences in North American and overseas.

Suzanne was hired to create and edit the *Vineyard Newsletter*, for Vineyard churches. She is a talented writer and editor. The Vineyard church movement was in its infant stage, the natural though unplanned growth from John Wimber's catalytic and explosive ministry. John had no intention of starting a denomination. But he came under immense pressure from leaders all over North America and overseas to transition the movement to a more structured organization. I remember sitting in on a meeting with John and C. Peter Wagner where Peter said, "If you begin to develop structures to bring oversight to these churches, you will only be able to maintain personal control until you reach 200 congregations. Then, even if you do not call it a denomination, it will be one." Peter pleaded with John to avoid starting what someday would be a denomination. He knew that most denominations don't make room for prophets, even their founding prophets. The prophet is too innovative, risk taking, unpredictable for organizations run by administrators and bureaucrats. There is no place for nonconformists.

John was uncomfortable starting a church movement with formal membership. Through the 1980s, he received requests from leaders wanting to convert their congregations to Vineyards or plant a new Vineyard church. He resisted.

A church movement presented two problems. First, John's appeal to leaders from different traditions was augmented by his

not intentionally recruiting leaders or churches into a new denomination. In other words, he was non-threatening. When the Association of Vineyard Churches was birthed and started growing, John's
appeal to other Christian groups waned. Second, a growing church
association needed administrative oversight, and with it the political and power struggles for control that plague all denominations.
The Vineyard movement was led by many musicians and artists,
unique in church history. Denominations are led by administrators
and bureaucrats, not the most creative people.

I heard the problem described this way: First, there is the man,
someone with a unique calling to his generation. Soon men follow
the man—his vision and values—and the influence of the man
spreads like wildfire; the men then organize and start a movement. The movement evolves into a machine of men who eventually erect monuments celebrating the good old days. The man,
the men, the movement, the monument—this lifecycle happens
quickly, and John knew it. And once the process started, it became
a runaway train.

When the Vineyard became a denomination, Vineyard leadership conferences lost much of their broad international appeal, and
John's voice waned in the movement he founded. Today, the Vineyard denomination has over 2,400 congregations worldwide. Many
of the leaders know neither who John Wimber was nor his vision
and values. Typical of most denominations, its early dynamic
expansion period is a faint memory.

The Vineyard of the 1980s was a movement transitioning to
a machine of men. Like Peter Wagner, I would have preferred
that John remained focused on the equipping ministry, leadership
development, and music. He could still coach church planters,
avoiding the burdens of governmental oversight. But that was my

opinion, and I was called to serve and submit to John. That was my Big Word, so I supported the Vineyard transition to a denominational structure.

Marriage Weekends

Obeying Big Words opens new and unexpected opportunities to ministry. I came to California to write books, but God had much more in mind. That's what makes hearing and obeying God's voice an adventure. Obedience often creates new, unimagined opportunities.

In 1989, John approached Suzanne and me, proposing we start a marriage renewal ministry. "I've been praying, and I see you bringing strength and healing to marriages." John was concerned about the deterioration of many leaders' and members' marriages in the Vineyard movement. There was little understanding of the biblical foundations for marriage, roles, sexuality, and such basic skills as communication and conflict resolution.

Suzanne and I had never considered a marriage ministry, but as we prayed, we sensed it might be God's will. Over the years we had attended annual events to strengthen our own marriage—seminars and conferences. We believed we should invest at least as much time and money in our marriage as we do in the upkeep of our cars. We had also felt called to encourage young couples, often by leading couples' discipleship groups that inevitably focused on marriage. As we reflected on our years of counseling couples, going back to Grace Haven in Mansfield, we realized God was preparing us to take a step of faith and start a marriage ministry. John's word was a Big Word from God.

We designed weekends with several key elements. For example, we were dual microphoned and stood next to each other, so couples could hear and see the husband wife dynamic as we talked side by side. They not only heard Suzanne's words when she spoke, they could *see* my response—my body language. They could hear our frequent inserts to give a husband's or wife's insight. We wanted to model healthy and respectful communication in our presentations. If the couples left the weekend only with precepts and principles, we failed to get to the heart of marriage. This meant Suzanne and I needed to be transparent about our marriage—the good, the bad, the sometimes ugly but usually entertaining disclosures.

So our presentations were highly interactive and, as it turned out, unintentionally quite funny at times. I fell into the straight role; Suzanne delivered the punch lines—but always with a higher purpose. Suzanne came alive in the weekends. She was relaxed, dynamic, and insightful. Husbands needed to hear and see Suzanne, so they could better understand their wives; and wives needed to observe me to better understand the man in their life.

The weekends were much more than talking heads. After each presentation, carefully designed to last from twenty-five to forty minutes, the couples were given a partner project to encourage them to apply what they were learning. We avoided group inter-actions: the weekend was for the couple and only the couple. Any interaction with others was casual, usually over a meal.

The content of our first weekend, developed with Van and Joyce Pewthers, was titled "Marriage with a Purpose." Most couples have little understanding of God's purposes for their marriage. We defined what love in marriage looks like, and four specific pur-poses outlined in scripture. These were the foundational talks for the event. The subsequent sessions focused on how to live out love and purpose. We covered the basics: communication, conflict res-olution, a husband loving his wife and a wife loving her husband, sex, forgiveness, and finally inviting the Holy Spirit into marriage for blessing and empowerment. Personal prayer for each couple climaxed the event.

There were many incredible stories of restoration; I'll recount only one here. During the Saturday evening session of an Anaheim weekend in 1992, a couple who had been married approximately ten years approached us. They were not doing well. The wife looked defeated, and the husband bewildered. He said, "I love my wife so much, and I don't know what I've done wrong. She won't tell me. I will do anything to bring her back to me." Paralyzed with guilt and fear, she barely spoke; so we asked the husband to wait in another part of the room. He complied, walking to a far, lonely corner. Then, with tears in her eyes, she shared that before they married, she lied to her husband, assuring him she had never slept with a man. In their culture (they were Asian immigrants), that was a marriage nullifier. Their marriage started out well, but soon creeping guilt and shame caused her to withdraw and shut down emotionally and sexually. "In our culture," she said, "If I tell my husband the truth, he must divorce me. But I love him and can't stand the thought of losing him." Suzanne and I asked if she had a relationship with Christ. "Yes!" And your husband? "Yes, very much so." "Then you are now under a new kingdom and have come into a new culture." She didn't believe us, but she was desperate, likely headed toward an emotional breakdown. So she asked, "What should I do?" "You must tell your husband. Now. Tonight. We will pray for you as you confess to him. You must tell him the truth and trust Christ."

She sucked up the little courage and faith she had—I thought she was going to faint—turned and walked across the room toward her husband, who moved toward her. We watched them from afar. All we could see was her animated hand movement from the back, which culminated with them dropping limp to her side and her head lowered in shame, guilt, and utter defeat. But it lasted less than a second. He threw his arms around her, pulled her close to his heart, and held her in a way that said he would never let her go. Her tears of shame turned to fountains of joy. Honesty, repentance, forgiveness, and the presence of God worked a miracle. The next morning, they sat in the front row, holding on to each other like newlyweds. Their emotional and sexual damage was healed by God's grace. Christ is in the culture-changing business.

We planned four events in southern California, promoting them through a brochure. Our first weekend, with fifty couples, was at a local Embassy Suites. Another marriage weekend in Indian Wells at the Hyatt Grand Champions had over one hundred couples attend. That was the last time we promoted the marriage ministry. Soon we were invited to speak around North America and Great Britain, even outside Vineyard circles. We relied solely on word of mouth, conducting some fifty events over the following ten years. We also developed a second weekend with Van and Joyce, titled "Enjoying the Differences," focusing on male, female, personality, and family of origin differences.

After conducting a weekend in San Francisco in September of 1996 at a Catholic retreat center, a woman approached us with a proposal. A corporate event planner, she thought a secular version of our teaching would be a big hit at executive retreats. "Frequently they bring their spouses and want an enrichment element for couples. You would be perfect, speaking a couple times during the weekend." She was impressed with Suzanne, who connected with both men and women in the audience. She especially liked the "Sex in Marriage" session, in which Suzanne was the primary speaker. "Also, these corporate events would pay big money for someone like you, very different from how churches pay." Our financial goal was only to cover expenses; the idea of being paid a lot of money for speaking never entered our minds. We did not seriously consider her proposal. Removing Christ from the weekend would be like removing a heart from the body and expecting it to live.

Dealing with Death

In June 1991, after playing 18 holes of golf, enjoying coffee with his Spudnuts Donuts buddies, and spending a quiet evening with my mother, my father went to bed and died from chronic heart failure in his sleep. Bill was seventy-four years old. Dad was a good man who loved God, his wife, and his four children. More than anything, he was kind. Eight-hundred people attended his memorial service at Calvary Community Church in Westlake Village, California, where for years mom and dad served as greeters. Everyone knew and loved dad. He lived up to his Noble name.

Dad's death kicked off a new era in my life: dealing with the death of loved ones. My mother, already unstable, quickly deteriorated without dad's care. In March 1992, Mom spent several days with us in Yorba Linda; she was obviously depressed. Suzanne and I pleaded with her to see a psychologist that we had lined up back in Westlake Village. I even offered to drive up to her home and take her to the doctor for each appointment, but she adamantly refused. As a pastor I had observed that men and women of her generation—the so-called Greatest Generation—rarely talked about the deeper emotions and hurts that debilitated them. I even called a pastor at her church, asking if he or someone would encourage her to seek help. I discovered they already had reached out, but she resisted. "I'm just fine," she said. "No problems."

On August 19, 1992, less than two years after my father died, mom committed suicide. Elizabeth Ann Springer not only confessed faith in Christ, but she was also instrumental in my coming into a personal relationship with him, practically pushing me on the bus that took me to hear Billy Graham speak at the Los Angeles Memorial Coliseum. I struggled greatly with how she died and continue to do so to this day. Writing these memoirs has helped me to understand her, especially the painful experiences of her childhood. I have confidence that Christ's eternal sacrifice on the cross more than covered mom's shortcomings, and I look forward to seeing her again in eternity.

On May 20, 1993, Suzanne's father Bob passed away after a long struggle with an unusual blood disorder and related heart disease. He was seventy-eight years old. Unlike my mother's and father's deaths, Bob's death was not surprising. Bob, who appropriately questioned my ability to provide for his daughter before we married, had become one of my biggest supporters. We became close over the years. I especially loved spending vacations with him in Manzanillo, Mexico, their second home for six months a year, listening to his World War II and Ford Motor Corporation stories. He loved our children, and they adored him, their "Boppo." Many of Suzanne's finest character traits come from her father.

In two years, we lost three of our four parents. Only Suzanne's mother Phyllis remained, and she was in good health. For that I was grateful because she had become the mother I never experienced—wise, strong, and generous. Phyllis was thoroughly converted to Christ, emotionally and relationally mature. She and Bob had even planted a small, expatriate church in Manzanillo. Suzanne and I knew we were entering a new chapter of life. Change was coming, like it or not.

Back to Pastoring

In 1992, John Wimber became ill with a brain tumor, which severely limited his stamina. He was already cutting back on his conference schedule and travel, and now he was not able to adequately pastor the Anaheim Vineyard Christian Fellowship. The church had moved into a new twenty-four-million-dollar building that seated 3,300. John was concerned about the church as it went through a major transition. He asked senior associate pastors Carl Tuttle and Bill Twyman to oversee the church, and then he approached me, asking if I would be willing to serve as an associate pastor. I did not want to do it, but God's Big Word said I was to serve, submit, and be loyal to John, so I obeyed from my heart.

Carl and Bill both wanted to be the next senior pastor of the Anaheim Vineyard, and they admitted it to me. I had no interest, for a variety of reasons. First, I was not qualified to pastor a megachurch—usually defined as having over 2,000 in attendance. I once asked John the key characteristic to being a megachurch pastor. Without hesitating he responded, "One word: *ruthless*. A megachurch pastor must be ruthless." Coming from John the idea of being ruthless was ironic because he was tough but not ruthless. By ruthless John certainly didn't mean brutal, inhumane, or unforgiving, qualities usually associated with ruthlessness. He meant singularly focused on your calling, never falling into the trap of people pleasing. In other words, ruthless with yourself.

Second, the church's finances were shaky at best. The debt on the building was massive, over twelve million dollars. VMI and Vineyard Music Group underwrote the church's budget, but with John retiring their continuing support was threatened. Further, the staff was bloated, needing to be cut and restructured—not an easy job. Staff insecurities were running high; men and women were anxious about their futures. Well they should have been insecure, because the church needed a new leader who would be willing to make tough changes to prepare the people for their next stage of growth without John.

Third, whoever followed John Wimber would always be compared to John Wimber. It was hard enough being nicknamed "*with Kevin Springer*" by Peter Wagner, because that's how I was listed on the cover of our books. I could not imagine being compared to John every Sunday in front of thousands of people.

Fourth, my Big Word was to serve John until he retired, then I'd be free to pursue God's next adventure for our lives. I could live with that.

Finally, and most significantly, I was not called to be the pastor of the Anaheim Vineyard. No Big Word. No desire. Absolutely no sense of calling from God.

For a year and a half, I served a congregation in limbo, hoping for John's return. During my tenure I oversaw small groups, men's discipleship, creative evangelistic outreaches, and even developed a new Saturday Night Celebration service. John named Carl Tuttle the senior pastor. Carl asked me to serve as his executive pastor. I declined Carl's offer, because I have neither the administrative gifts nor desire to be an effective executive pastor.

At that point, John announced his retirement. My time in Anaheim had come to an end. I had fulfilled my assignment. Now what?

EIGHT

Springs in the Desert

Palm Desert, California

*"When once the call of God comes,
begin to go and never stop going."*
—Oswald Chambers, *My Utmost for His Highest*

When John Wimber announced his retirement, I was set free. But set free to do what? I needed a Big Word from God.

I never sat around waiting for a Big Word from God, and I have never chased after prophets asking for a prophetic word. Instead, I followed the advice Augustine of Hippo wrote in his homily on 1 John 4:4–12, "Once for all, then, a short precept is given thee: Love, and do what thou wilt." Or, as I like to interpret it, "Love God and do what you want." Christ's greatest command is to "love God with all of our heart, soul, and mind" (Matthew 22:37). If my heart were conformed to God's love, what I chose to do would be his will for me. But what did I want to do next?

I have always been a pastor who writes, not a writer who pastors. I wanted to be a pastor. Having participated in starting two congregations, I was more comfortable planting a church than taking on an existing congregation. The challenge of starting and growing new works energizes me, and I prefer to avoid cleaning up other leaders' messes. My gift mix was made for church planting.

But where?

John Wimber encouraged Suzanne and me to pray about San Diego and the Coachella Valley—the latter included communities like Palm Springs and Palm Desert. He also committed to support us financially for six months if we decided to plant. We visited San Diego but had no peace to plant there. Palm Desert seemed to make sense for several reasons. Suzanne's mother owned a second home in the Palm Desert Tennis Club which she offered for transitional housing, and we were familiar with the area having vacationed in the desert over the years. There were also negatives. Two failed local Vineyard churches had left a bad taste in the mouths of many people. The more recent failure, of a church which at one time had over 500 attendees, was tainted with scandal of financial improprieties. In addition, the Coachella Valley was a seasonal resort area, and I was unsure about pastoring a congregation in which attendance could vary by 50 percent over the course of a year.

Not wanting to leave any rock unturned, I interviewed for a position at a Christian publishing company in Ventura. During the interview, which went well, one of their senior editors casually said, "I would love to work with you, but I'd be more interested in attending a church that you pastored." Sometimes Big Words come from off-handed remarks. I had not mentioned pastoring in the interview; her remark came out of left field. That was a confirming word from God. I was supposed to pastor.

York Minster Cathedral

In March 1994, Martyn and Linda Smith invited Suzanne and me to speak at a church in Manchester, England. We decided to stay an extra week in York to celebrate our twenty-fifth wedding anniversary, on March 29. York is our most cherished place in Great Britain—an ancient, walled city that is the home of York Minster, one of the world's most magnificent cathedrals. We love walking on the city walls, poking through art shops and bookstores on narrow, cobble-stone streets, and savoring afternoon tea at Bettys Café Tea Rooms. But the highlight, bar none, is the cathedral. Praying in the Minster was home coming for me, returning to my Episcopal roots.

On March 29, 1994, while we were praying in the cathedral, God, in his still small voice, spoke to us through Scripture. He gave us Isaiah 43:19, which would become God's guiding word for the next twelve years of our lives: "I am about to do a brand-new thing. See, I have already begun! Do you not see it? I will make a pathway through the wilderness for my people to come home. I will create rivers for them in the desert!" We were to go to Palm Desert.

The Big Word was clear. First, God said, "I am about to do a brand-new thing." This will be a church plant. Second, he said, "See, I have already begun! Do you not see it?" God was already plowing the ground, so to speak, before we even moved to Palm Desert. Suzanne and I would need eyes of faith to see God's preparation and provision for a new work that would glorify him. Third, he said, "I will make a pathway through the wilderness for my people to come home." This church plant was to be a place for people who feel lost and discouraged to come home; a place where their spiritual thirst would be quenched by God's word (John 4:10–14), living water from the well of salvation which brings eternal life (Isaiah 12:3), and the refreshing of the Holy Spirit (John 7:37–39).

Having heard God's voice in York, we returned home committed to planting in Palm Desert. We knew our next move would come at a great cost. Jesus taught "the kingdom of heaven is a like a merchant in search of fine pearls, who, on finding one pearl of great value, went and sold all that he had and bought it" (Matthew 13:45–46). Obedience to Big Words frequently costs everything, and this was no different.

As Suzanne prayed, she heard God's voice: Palm Desert was our pearl of great price. So, we fell to our knees and prayed an official prayer—as we call it—sacred prayer that we agree on. "Lord," we prayed, "We are sold out." We were not rich, but we had saved some money. Suzanne sensed we needed to be committed to putting everything we owned on the line, until we got down to our last $10,000.

March 29, 1994, at the York Minster Cathedral (York, England)
where we received a Big Word to plant a church in Palm Desert, California

More Christians, Better Christians

In 1994, I was forty-six years old and had a clear vision of what the new church, which would be called Desert Springs (naturally), would be. Simply summarized, I said, "We are called to make more Christians and better Christians." That was the vision, and I would implement it through my gifts as a catalytic leader, evangelist, and teacher. My strategy was to build a foundation of healthy, strong believers, particularly focusing on discipling men. The typical evangelical church is 60 to 70 percent women. I intended to initiate a church that was evenly balanced between women and men. Every church I have pastored has been equally divided between men and women; we never suffered a dearth of dynamic women leaders. Churches that have strong, healthy men tend to have strong, healthy women.

Many church plants fail because they are overwhelmed by unhealthy people, folks with serious emotional and relational problems. In Scripture the church is compared to an army (winning the lost), a school (making and maturing disciples), and a hospital (a healing center). But church plants that become only MASH (Mobile Army Surgical Hospital) units quickly burn out their small leadership core. A long-term strategy builds on health.

When we returned from York, we told John Wimber about our Big Word from Isaiah 43:19. We were called to Palm Desert. He agreed. He also agreed to come to the desert on July 29, 1994, and apologize on behalf of the Vineyard for the two failed Vineyard churches that had left many hurt and angry believers in their wake. At this meeting of roughly 300 people, John laid hands on Suzanne and me and blessed us. John's blessing for favor and protection was integral to our future success.

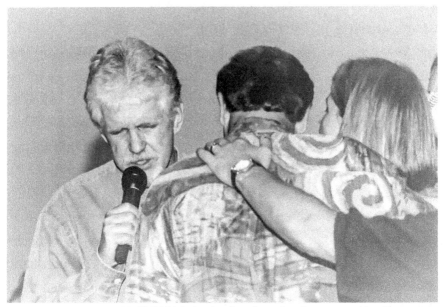

July 29, 1994, John lays hands on Suzanne and me,
blessing us and the church plant in Palm Desert, California

John also encouraged us to meet with Trevor (not his real name) an older pastoral leader who led a group of about seventy-five believers in the Coachella Valley. This was meant to be a courtesy call only. Trevor was a retired major league baseball player—successful in his day—who cut his spiritual teeth under Aimee Semple McPherson at Angelus Temple, a megachurch in Los Angeles. She was the founder of the Foursquare Church, a Pentecostal denomination. Our theological and ecclesiological backgrounds could not be more disparate. Suzanne and I met Trevor and his gracious wife in their home at PGA West. After recounting several of his remarkable baseball stories (I loved them!), he said, "Yup, you are the ones. God told me what I have I am to give to you." I explained to him that we did not want his congregation, but if he wanted to recommend that individually they become a part of our new congregation we would be willing to meet with them. Approximately fifty adults affiliated with Trevor would be a part of the beginning of the church plant.

Through the spring and early summer, I commuted weekly the one hundred miles from Yorba Linda to Palm Desert, meeting with a core of seven or eight couples. My purpose was to clarify our vision and values. On one of those commutes from Yorba Linda in July 1994, God spoke yet another Big Word. Driving up Monterey Avenue through the star-lit night of the desert, I noticed a church building on the right side of the road and heard God say, "One day you are going to have a church on Monterey Avenue in Palm Desert." This was another confirming word, two months before the church launched, that God called us to Palm Desert. There was no doubt in my mind that someday we would be meeting in the building I just saw.

Coming and Going

We had far more people than those affiliated with Trevor. Like any new church, most people come with differing expectations and agendas. Desert Springs was no different. Most of the early participants held strong opinions about who John Wimber was, expecting me to be the mini-John of their imaginations. This presented two challenges. First, John Wimber was not the person they thought he was. They had little idea of his core values and vision, usually projecting their values onto him. In fact, almost none of them had ever met John. Second, even if I wanted to be John, I could not. I was Kevin Noble Springer, with my unique personality, background, and gifting.

New churches, like newborn babies, are vulnerable. The first year went as expected, an ebb and flow growing to 150 attendance. Many of the folks associated with Trevor filtered out while new people replaced them. We blessed those who left, including Trevor's son-in-law who took a small group and started a new church. I liked him, and after that we occasionally met over coffee at Espresso-to-a-Tea.

John Wimber once told me, "Love the people while they are passing through. We are all just passing through." Church planters need strong constitutions for all the coming and going, the criticism and rejection.

Church plants are also like new restaurants—the majority fail. As I clarified our vision, people with competing visions and agendas dropped out while others were drawn in. We were also growing with new Christians, an integral characteristic of spiritual health.

The Traveling Prophet

Most new congregations are targets for hostile take-overs. Desert Springs was no different. About a year into our history a lovely couple approached me to inquire about a traveling prophet speaking at the church. I asked them a few questions, then said, "No. I don't know him. I do not know his message. He's traveling alone apart from his wife and children, which is a red flag. I would no more let him speak at Desert Springs than I would let a stranger— or any other man—sleep with my wife. I have a responsibility to protect the congregation." They understood, but still wanted him to speak. So they asked how I felt about them opening their large home to invite friends to hear him. "I have no right or authority to say no to that, as long it is not a church event. But I want to remind you that 1 John 4:1 says, 'Do not believe every spirit, but test the spirits to see whether they are from God, for many false prophets have gone out into the world.'"

There was a hunger for prophetic ministry, so their home was packed. After hearing reports about the meetings for a few days, Suzanne said, "I need to go check on this. Some of our people are attending." During the meeting, the prophet said, "I see Pastor Kevin's wife Suzanne, and the Lord has told me they are leaving Palm Desert soon." Much to her credit, Suzanne immediately responded, "No, you have that wrong. Very wrong. We are called here and are committed for the long term." He turned red with anger; he was planting a seed of doubt about our calling and commitment.

A few days later, he was accused of assaulting two women, one of whom attended Desert Springs Church. The other woman was the recently divorced adult daughter of a pastor in another town. The traveling prophet was a powerfully built man who could overpower most women. The women chose not to involve the police. The pastor from the nearby town and I met with about forty people who had attended the meetings. A few were receptive to our pastoral direction, many were not. The couple who opened their home were saddened but solid in standing for righteousness. They remain friends to this day. Biblical wisdom and discernment averted a potential crisis with the prophet.

There might not be a more difficult calling than being a pastor. You preach the gospel, asking people to turn ownership of their lives over to Christ; then you disciple them to think differently about *everything*; next you train them to serve and give them assignments inside and outside the congregation. Finally, you ask them to write a tithe check and give it to the church to advance the gospel. It is an impossible task apart from the God's leading, power, and intervention.

Change and Challenge

Desert Springs continued to grow, which meant hiring pastoral and support staff and building a leadership structure to cover music, children and youth, women's and men's ministries, seniors, the poor, missions, and office administration. Jette Lai, my secretary at the Anaheim Vineyard, wanted to be a part of the church plant. She volunteered to be the church's first secretary. I had met Brad Swope in Anaheim, and he became our first staff pastoral hire. Soon we had offices, more pastors and workers, and a leadership infrastructure. I also needed to develop a board to oversee our finances. According to the Desert Springs polity, I was accountable to the board, and staff reported to me.

The most difficult hire in a new church usually is the pastor of music, or worship pastor. Because we were a Vineyard, the music bar was set high. Many people come to a Vineyard church for the music and hang around for the message. The first few months we recruited visiting worship leaders from around southern California, hoping to find a more permanent leader. In 1995, we called a worship leader from the Midwest, Bob Baker, a man of high character, who moved his wife and five children to Palm Desert. This was a financial strain on the church and his family. Sometimes the best people do not make the right fit. Bob returned home. We even brought in a young worship intern, hoping he could fill the gap. Unfortunately he wasn't a good fit. After more than a year, we were still looking, and I was discouraged.

Eventually a more experienced worship leader filled out our team. His style was what we were looking for at that time. He was gifted and charismatic. The new worship leader had an immediate impact. Sunday music came alive. Even Natalie Cole, when performing in Palm Springs, worshipped at Desert Springs Church. Our other hires, from secretaries and sound crew to associate pastors and youth ministers, worked out well. However, the stress of managing a larger staff and dealing with the pressure of a growing budget took their toll on me. Our operating expenses, especially the money needed to meet our monthly obligations, kept me on my knees.

Impact '97

Sometimes Big Words make absolutely no sense at the time they are given, which was the case for me in 1990 when God planted a seed in my heart that would transform Desert Springs Church seven years later.

Don Swearingen and I attended Ashland Theological Seminary in the early 1970s and maintained a robust friendship over the years. In 1989 Don heard about a church growth phone campaign called Phones for You, and decided to start a new church using their strategy. After recruiting a small leadership core in Columbus, Ohio, Don's team made 20,000 calls in his community, asking those who were not attending a church if they would be interested in learning more about a new congregation. Around 2,000 unchurched people expressed interest—some only casual curiosity—and provided their addresses. After sending a series of high quality but simple mailings over a few weeks, they were invited to a special Sunday service. A few days before the first service, the most effective phoners from the previous phase gave one more personal touch to those showing interest. On Don Swearingen's inaugural Sunday, over 200 people showed up—almost every person unchurched with minimal if any faith. Less than a year later, the church closed its doors. If this sounds like a telemarketing disaster for Jesus, it was.

Because he was a friend, I asked Don if he learned anything from his costly experiment. "Yes. We had almost no leadership structure or ability to disciple the new people who made commitments to Christ. So you need a church before you grow a church."

And then God spoke a Big Word to me: "One day you will do Phones for You in a church you pastor, and it will change everything." It was not a word I wanted to hear. Besides, I wasn't pastoring a church in 1990. But I knew it was a word from God.

In the second year of our church plant, I believed the time was ripe to reach out to the unchurched in Palm Desert and asked the staff to pray. In June 1996, I attended a men's Promise Keepers gathering in San Diego and happened to sit next to a pastor who recently successfully completed a phone campaign like Phones for You. I set up a meeting with him later that summer to investigate, remembering the Big Word from 1990. By 1996, Desert Springs had developed a leadership core, infrastructure, and pastoral systems for disciple making. Don had said, "You need a church to grow a church." Well, we had a church.

In September, I presented the Desert Springs staff with a proposal to reach the unchurched: Phones for You. None of the staff was excited about participating in what felt like a telemarketing campaign. I then asked Brad Swope to coordinate the project, and he reluctantly agreed. When Brad read the material from Phones for You, the Holy Spirit put a fire in his heart to live out the Great Commission—to go and make disciples of Christ in Palm Desert. In early October, the staff caught and bought the vision, and we named the outreach Impact '97. By November the entire congregation, now averaging 300 Sunday attendance, started to mobilize for the outreach.

Every Sunday I would cast the vision: we are called to make more Christians and better Christians, which means God is not calling Desert Springs Church to grow from church transfers. God calls us to reach out boldly to the lost and unchurched with the gospel of truth and hope in Christ. We aren't building a better mouse trap for the already saved; we are building a refuge for those who hunger for God.

The atmosphere in the church was electric. There was a renewed faith to reach out. One member came forward and volunteered their large, direct-marketing phone bank room. Brad organized six teams of eager volunteers—from set-up crews for a special tent to mailing teams. One hundred trained members made 37,000 calls over a four week period in January. Over 3,700 people said they wanted to learn more and immediately were mailed a postcard thanking them for their interest and reminding them of what they were to receive and when. In all, over two-hundred Desert Springs members enthusiastically participated.

What I did not expect was how the process of the outreach changed the Desert Springs Church. Many members who made calls left the phone bank in tears, saying they shared the gospel with more people in one night than in their entire lives. The calls were only to invite unchurched people to visit Desert Springs, but sometimes complete strangers opened their hearts over the phones. I led a local contractor to Christ during one call. He later said it was a miracle because he turned off the Oakland Raiders' football game—he was a football fanatic—to talk about God. Perhaps the biggest miracle of all was that out of 37,000 calls we received only one complaint.

On March 2, 1997, Desert Springs hosted over 200 first-time visitors, most of whom were not attending church elsewhere. Six-hundred people in total attended the service that Sunday, and the church was ready to welcome them. First-time visitors continued to come over the following weeks. I preached a series of messages on "How to Choose a Church," and they kept coming back. By the beginning of April, our average attendance topped 500, with many new believers. True to the Big Word, everything changed.

My Last Visit with John Wimber

John Wimber's health continued to deteriorate, and by July 1997, I was hearing discouraging reports of his chances for making it through the year. In August I visited him at his mountain home in Lake Arrowhead. He did not look well. We sat on his back porch and talked, mostly about our era working together and the general state of the Vineyard. For several years he had felt uneasy about the Vineyard's direction. During a conference at the Anaheim Convention Center back in 1993, he confided to me, "This doesn't feel like my Vineyard anymore." The equipping and evangelism focus that marked his early ministry had been replaced by prophets and healing evangelists from other ministry streams. This was a difficult time for him. Shortly after our visit his health began to fail, and with it his strength and vitality faded.

The halcyon days of the Vineyard were over, and he knew there was no turning back. In my opinion, his poor health clouded his thinking as he struggled with regrets that he failed to keep the Vineyard grounded in its founding vision and values. I strongly disagreed with him, reminding him that all renewal movements have a short shelf life, perhaps ten or fifteen years. Now is time for the next generation to carry on, for better or worse. He had no control over what they would do. I encouraged him to let it go. John Wimber was a good and faithful servant. I believe when he died, he was ready to go into Christ's presence.

God's timing is perfect, never too soon and never too late. Psalm 139:16 says, "Your eyes saw my unformed substance; in your book were written, every one of them, the days that were formed for me, when as yet there was none of them." John's days were numbered. November 17, 1997 was the last one. A true friend went to his well-deserved rest in paradise. I suspect trumpets were playing.

Location, Location, Nine Locations

One of the greatest challenges for most new congregations is where to meet. At the beginning Desert Springs had almost immediately encountered a facility crisis. We started in the gym at a private Christian school, an ideal complex but in a terrible location. After a few weeks, the headmaster of the school informed me that another church with better funding than Desert Springs wanted the gym. Besides, he said, he did not think we would last. "Don't take it personally. It's just a business decision." Without any notice, we were out on the street. The next week we met at the Desert Springs Marriott Resort. (The church that replaced us failed within two years.)

That began a nomadic odyssey for the next seven years in which we met at the Rancho Mirage Country Club, the Palm Desert Community Center, the Oasis Adventist Church, and a middle school. We even met for several months in a tent that Rick Warren had used at Saddleback Church in Orange County. In all, we moved *nine* times. I used to say, "Desert Springs is a great church, if you can find us." Frequent moves created a feeling of instability and impermanence, were costly, stressful, and hindered growth. But they also created opportunities for courageous steps of faith, creative thinking, and big risks. Afterall, what did we have to lose? Every fall a seasonal attendee would confide to me, "I was wondering if you would even be here when I returned." More than one visitor told me, "I'd attend this church if you had a permanent home."

Temple Sinai

The demographics of Palm Desert and the surrounding cities of Rancho Mirage, Indian Wells, and La Quinta are a mix of wealthy, older seasonal residents and younger folk—teachers, business-people, contractors, golf professionals, and restaurant owners and workers. A significant percentage of the homes in the central valley are in gated communities, many of them exclusive country clubs. There are over 120 golf courses in the Coachella Valley, the great-est concentration of courses in the country.

By 1999, we needed a building in Palm Desert if we were to keep growing. Back in 1994, God said that we would "have a building on Monterey in Palm Desert," and I thought it was the church I saw that starry night. When I informed the pastoral staff that we needed to start looking for a building, they almost laughed me out of the room. One said, "We don't even have enough money to scholarship men to our annual retreat." He was right about our finances, but wrong about God's will. My confidence was rooted in God's word, not our bank account.

I never cared much about money, and probably didn't pay as much attention to it as I should have. Ideas, big ideas from God, have always been my primary motivation. If I could be part of a community that makes more Christians and better Christians, money would take care of itself. For that to happen, Desert Springs needed a church home.

I had recruited the church's board for integrity, loyalty, wisdom, and gifting, especially in financial management and administrative matters. They were strong where I was weak; I was good at raising money, not as gifted managing it. The board consisted of a highly respected attorney, a successful businessman, the Rancho Mirage city engineer, an experienced builder, the president of Palm Desert

Bank, and a retired American Baptist area pastoral overseer. Our treasurer was the CFO of the Eisenhower Hospital system, a CPA by training. The board had more faith for a building than the staff, agreeing strongly that we should pursue buying one. They were confident that God would provide the money.

Most new churches take about twelve years before buying their first building. Desert Springs pursued its first building in year six. Once the decision to buy was made, the church mobilized to search out locations, design budgets, determine financial goals, and raise money. My job became more complicated and challenging—meetings, fundraising, strategic decisions, and pastoring many people with different opinions about the new building. Potentially large donors are the key to successful building campaigns; I needed to spend time with them, explaining the Desert Spring's vision and answering their questions. More experienced pastors counseled me to delegate oversight of daily operations of the church to my staff. "I need to trust you to oversee the church," I told two key staffers, "while I oversee the building project. I will preach but won't be able to perform many other tasks."

Mike Kingsbury, the church treasurer, diligently worked at getting our books to pass an audit. This meant updated procedures and budget refinement. I supported him wholeheartedly. This was necessary to qualify for a substantial building loan from a lending institution. Desert Springs Church initiated a relationship with one of the largest church lending banks in the nation. We were dotting our *i*'s and crossing our *t*'s, paying meticulous attention to detail, which included departmental spending.

Our search soon led to a synagogue, Temple Sinai, which was up for sale in the heart of Palm Desert. Not as large a building as we wanted, it was what we could afford. Young churches, like young families, buy starter homes—then as they grow, they move up. Many churches take on unreasonable debt, and soon their financial burdens determine ministry decisions. Desert Springs never wanted financial need to control ministry priorities.

The capital campaign went well, but not as well as it should have. The staff that I trusted to oversee the church no longer agreed with the vision of the church, buying the synagogue, or my leadership. They were very unhappy, openly talking to junior staff and church members about their dissatisfaction. Being busy with sermon preparation, overseeing the capital campaign and other building concerns, I was unaware of their unhappiness, though I saw signs of discord growing in the church.

Concerned for my staff, I wanted the best for them, even if they needed to move on. So I asked one of them to spend a day with me in Idyllwild, a mountain hamlet about an hour from Palm Desert. "Let's walk and talk and pray in the woods. I want to hear you out." He told me he thought his time at Desert Springs was coming to an end, and said he was looking into moving to another state. I tried to encourage him, saying he had a good tenure at Desert Springs but needed to finish well.

In every transition Suzanne and I have gone through, we have never burned bridges, maintaining friendships from past ministries for decades. I asked how I could support him in his next posting. What was troubling him? Among other things, he disagreed with the church government; he was especially distressed by the board's authority over me—and indirectly him. "What if they fired you tomorrow?" he asked. "I'd step down," I answered, "believing it is God's will. That's the deal with our calling. When we commit our lives to serve Christ, we relinquish our rights. If I'm going to be a man in authority, I need to be under authority." He had other concerns, especially regarding my leadership, but he didn't articulate them that day. I greatly underestimated his discontentment. He asked to stay on staff until the church moved into its new home, which I agreed to. In retrospect, I made a mistake. It turned out not to be good for him, the church, or me.

God Works in Mysterious Ways

Monday of the week the synagogue escrow was scheduled to close, I received a call from the Christian lending institution that was making the purchase possible. We had spent over a year working with them, meeting their criteria, which was substantial. Our due diligence filled up a three-inch thick binder. "Kevin," the agent said, "I've got bad news. The board met and decided to turn down your loan. They think Desert Springs is a bad risk." Once again, I heard familiar words when he added, "Don't take it personally, it's just business. It is completely outside of my control. God bless you."

I was finished. The church was divided, with two key staff members saying buying the building was not God's will. I was also coping with the impending death of my younger brother, Scott, from cancer. Having lost my older brother two years earlier, also to cancer, this felt like a one-two punch. I was suffering with grief. And now this, the final nail in my pastoral coffin. "Lord," I prayed, "I don't understand what you are doing, but I trust you."

On Tuesday I met with our youth pastor, James Berteig, to tell him we were not purchasing the building, which necessitated my resignation. "James," I said, "You probably need to look for another position. I have booked a flight for myself to Minneapolis next week to talk with Larry Gehl (a seasonal church member and friend) about getting a job." In the middle of our conversation my phone rang. "Is this Pastor Kevin Springer?"

"Yes."

"This is Harvey Katofsky, the real estate agent for Temple Sinai, and I heard your loan was turned down yesterday and you won't be able to close on Friday. As you are aware, our purchase of the old Southwest Community Church building is dependent on your purchase of our temple this Friday. How much do you need?"

"Over $1,000,000."

"No problem. Go to the Berger Foundation and meet with their president, Ron Auen. They will loan you the money. He's expecting you."

"Uh, Okay."

Then he hung up. I didn't believe Harvey Katofsky, but what did I have to lose? So that afternoon I met with Ron Auen; the next day, Wednesday, Ron handed me the million-dollar-plus check. We closed on Temple Sinai on Thursday, one day early. Mr. Auen was not interested in looking at our due diligence, which strangely bothered me because Mike Kingsbury had worked so hard on it. "We are a foundation," Mr. Auen told me, "not a bank." He only required I bring in a board resolution approving the loan, signed by the secretary.

The Christians did not believe in us, but Harvey Katofsky and a secular foundation filled the gap. God works in mysterious ways.

A Mixed Blessing

Shortly after Temple Sinai was purchased, I met with one of the pastors who had become vehemently opposed to the building restoration plans and openly opposed my leadership. The meeting did not go well. He proposed disbanding the board and transferring all formal authority in the church to senior staff—to him, the other associate, and me. "We need security, and there is no security if you are submitted to the board. Why, they could fire you at any time for any reason." Soon after he and another pastor left Desert Springs, they took around one hundred people with them, diminishing our attendance when we moved into our new home just before Christmas. We also had residual losses that come with any church division. However, the church's income was not affected—most of the people who left were not financial givers. Further, almost every significant pastoral problem in the church ended after they left. In my final five years at Desert Springs, the church was unified, at peace, and grew annually.

The two former staff members also sued Desert Springs Church, serving the lawsuit at my home on Easter weekend in 2002. This legal action was disillusioning, though eventually the courts dismissed it without prejudice, which means the suit could never be brought again. I did not feel like a winner; instead, I was heartbroken for the body of Christ. Christ's reputation was tarnished. Everyone lost, especially the church. A few years later one of the pastors and I reconciled. I regularly bless him and his church in my prayers. He is my brother; how can I not ask God to bless his ministry? He proclaims Christ, and "in that I rejoice" (Philippians 1:18).

In Unity, Power Is Released

Those who stayed in Desert Springs, and they were a large majority, stepped up in service and commitment. I was a wounded warrior, and they surrounded Suzanne and me with love and support. The temple building needed extensive renovation. People like Don and Emma Howard, Larry and Sharon Gehl, John and Sandra Hartfield, Tom Anderson, Milt McKenzie, Christine Blydenburgh, the staff, and many others filled the gap. Their dedication was remarkable.

My brother Scott died on December 21, just after we celebrated the grand opening of the new building on December 16, 2001. Scott was one of my biggest spiritual and prayer supporters, and he was able to rejoice in the building opening before going to be with Christ. I barely got through Dedication Sunday, overcome with grief over the impending loss of my brother, and the absence of a few friends, even people I had led to a relationship with Christ and discipled. "God," I told the congregation, "deserves all the glory for this building. He alone provided, and now Desert Springs has a bright future. On March 29, 1994, the Lord promised, 'I am about to do a brand-new thing. See, I have already begun! Do you not see it? I will make a pathway through the wilderness for my people to come home. I will create rivers for them in the desert!'"

God did it. God began it; God made a pathway for his people; God created living waters in the desert. To God and only God be the glory.

Resignation Denied

When we obey Big Words, life becomes a magnificent tapestry. God wastes nothing, especially our failures and suffering. Joseph, after he was betrayed by his brothers, said, "You intended to harm me, but God intended it for good to accomplish what is now being done, the saving of many lives" (Genesis 50:20, NIV).

Paul wrote to the Corinthians, "Therefore, my dear brothers, be steadfast, immovable, always abounding in the work of the Lord, knowing that in the Lord your labor is not in vain" (1 Corinthians 15:58). I was tired but determined to remain steadfast in fulfilling God's Big Word for me, to keep on keeping on. To borrow a golfing term, God had me in his sweet spot.

My unimagined adventures of walking with Christ by following Big Words met resistance from the world, the flesh, and the devil—the three enemies of the soul. Obeying Big Words does not exempt one from hardship. My experience in Palm Desert can best be described as a dance of punch, counterpunch, and then rest. Frequently the punches left me dazed. But I kept getting up off the canvas and moving forward. God used the ups and downs for my good. He was teaching me total dependance on him.

In January 2002, I tendered my resignation to the Desert Springs board for allowing discord and division in the congregation. One of the primary callings of a shepherd is to protect the flock. I had failed, badly. The board met, and the next day answered me: "You are our pastor. We voted you an annual raise. Now get back to work." Suzanne and I fell to our knees and thanked God, trusting him for the future. In faith, I carried on.

After the board told me to get back to work, I analyzed what needed to change in the church. When I looked at the budget it became clear we had forgotten our commitment to missions and the poor. So, I repented to the church in a Sunday message, challenging us to put the poor and missions high in our hearts and wallets. We helped mobilize care for migrant farm workers' children in the east end of the Coachella Valley and donated financially to a homeless shelter. We also evaluated our missions' budget and supported works in Guinea-Bissau (one of the poorest nations in the world), Ecuador, and France, sending short-term mission teams to all three countries. God used the team that went to rural Guinea-Bissau to convert an entire village to Christ, and a revival radiated out to neighboring villages. By 2003, a significant percent of our total budget was committed to the poor and missions. I am convinced that this is the secret to Desert Springs Church's growth and prosperity in the remainder of my tenure. God was good indeed.

How a church cares for its weakest members is a proverbial canary in a coal mine, a bird who dies when methane gas is present, thus alerting miners to danger. Suzanne and I tried to look for men or women, usually single adults, who were alone and struggling with seemingly insurmountable problems—spiritual, medical, emotional, relational, financial. We quietly took them into our home, inviting them to experience the love of God and the health of our family life on special occasions. Christ was our model, mediating the presence of his father to whomever came into his life. We didn't do this for a reward, we acted out of gratitude for all that he did for us—we are all broken people in need of God's love and acceptance.

Lighthouse of the Valley

In 2001, during the period of greatest turmoil in the church, three local pastors reached out to support and encourage me. One pastor, Mike Coppersmith, from Our Savior's Community Lutheran Church in Palm Springs, had walked around the Desert Springs Church's future property several times late at night praying for me. His prayers, unknown to me at the time, were a primary reason I survived the attack. Mark Brattrud—pastor of Valley Christian Assembly, and Keith Newsome—who pastored a Christian Missionary Alliance church in Cathedral City, began meeting with me for encouragement and prayer. Soon Mike Coppersmith joined us. They were a lifeline.

Mike, Mark, Keith and I realized we needed each other, and we believed all the lead pastors in the Coachella Valley also needed each other. So, we approached Paul Cedar, who was chairman and CEO of the Mission America Coalition and living in the Coachella Valley, about helping to start a valley-wide ministerial association. Paul had previously served as President of the Evangelical Free Churches of America and had extensive experience as a pastor. He agreed to lead. We invited all the local pastors to meet at Desert Springs Church (because of our central location), and the Lighthouse of the Valley (LOV) movement was born. The LOV's vision is a partnership of evangelical churches and ministries to present the message of Jesus Christ to the valley. LOV has touched thousands of people, and even spread to other cities across the United States.

What started as three pastors supporting a hurting colleague turned into something beautiful for the kingdom. God wastes nothing.

Priorities Change

Even though the church was doing well, I was emotionally shot, desperately in need of help, healing, and refocusing. Anxiety debilitated me. I contacted my friend and colleague from Corona, pastor Bill Twyman, and he arranged counseling for me, and insisted on paying for it.

In one of our sessions, the counselor asked me, "Kevin, do you think God can get along without you?" "Uh," I responded sheepishly, "is that a trick question?" It was not. Having fallen into the trap of thinking Desert Springs, *Jesus'* church, could not get along without me was killing me emotionally. I had to let go, focus on what God called me to do, and let him take care of the rest. My priorities changed. Within a year, I made preaching, vision casting, and discipling men my top priorities. Administration and staff management went to the bottom of my to-do list.

In 2003, the church also called an executive pastor, Mark Cedar, Paul Cedar's son. A member of the church, over a round of golf, had told me he wanted to fully fund the position for three years. But who should we call? Unknown to me, Mark had been attending Desert Springs for several months when he applied for a pastoral position. At the time he did not know we were looking for an executive pastor. Mark was highly qualified, humble, and a perfect fit. My load became manageable.

In 2005, we conducted a low-key capital campaign to build phases two and three of our campus, a children's education building and a youth building. The funds were raised, and we broke ground.

Back in 1999, Tom Anderson had invited me to join his men's group, and I eagerly accepted. I was easily the youngest member, and I *wasn't* the leader, which was liberating. The group included Milt McKenzie, Higgins Bailey, and Ron Glosser. We met regularly for prayer, encouragement, and accountability in Tom's home in Palm Springs. Their support through the challenging times of unrest at Desert Springs was a key source of strength. Tom Anderson and Milt McKenzie were life changers for me.

Back in the sixteenth century St. John of the Cross wrote, "Love consists not in feeling great things but in having great detachment and in suffering for the Beloved." My identity in Christ had been compromised by making an idol of my calling. I needed great detachment from the church to complete my assignment at Desert Springs. Detachment does not imply uncaring, indifferent, or unloving attitudes toward the body of Christ. My efforts had to be subordinated completely to loving Christ. I would continue to suffer setbacks—some self-inflicted, some not—but by practicing the presence of Christ, they no longer controlled me. My last five years at Desert Springs were liberating.

A Red Herring

A few days after Christmas in 2004, the building I saw on Monterey Avenue when I received the Big Word on that starry night in 1994 became available. Bob Beaver, the pastor of the church and my friend, told me his congregation was so fractured and in debt it could not continue. I thought, "Well, perhaps I did hear God's voice back in 1994." We needed to build youth and children's centers at the temple location to meet the needs of an expanding congregation. The building that I saw back in 1994 had those facilities. John Hartfield and I met with the splintered remains of the congregation and made a purchase proposal. Their reception was hostile, for reasons that were never explained to us. When we left the meeting, John said, "No way, no how, do we want to touch this. We can't work with these people." He was right.

This plunged me into a different sort of crisis. "But God," I said, "I heard your voice. You said I'd have a church on Monterey Avenue in Palm Desert. I thought it was *this* church building, but it didn't materialize! You are my friend; I know your voice. What happened? What have I done wrong?" He didn't answer my questions, but I trusted him anyway.

In January of 2005, an acquaintance asked me where our new church was located. "On Monterey Avenue in Palm Desert, across from the entrance to the college." And then it hit me: I pastor a church *on Monterey Avenue in Palm Desert*. I *had* heard God's voice back in 1994 after all. If I had listened closely to his words, I would have known the building I thought we would buy could not be the one God intended for us, because it did not meet the criteria of the Big Word. That building was in the city of Rancho Mirage; the other side of Monterey Avenue was in Palm Desert. It was a red herring! The building we bought *was* in Palm Desert, on the Rancho Mirage border. In fact, other than a Mormon church, Temple Sinai was the *only* building on Monterey Avenue in Palm Desert that could fulfill the Big Word.

I *had* heard God's voice! But I learned something. When God speaks to you, listen very closely, and avoid jumping to hasty conclusions.

An Offer We Could Not Refuse

Two unexpected events happened at Desert Springs Church that would bless Suzanne's and my personal circumstances. The first was in 2001, when Mike Kingsbury, our church treasurer, informed the board that the federal government was allowing pastors who had previously opted out of Social Security to opt back in. I had unwisely opted out in 1972, thinking we were too poor to pay the taxes. (Well, we were too poor!) Apart from my knowledge, the Desert Springs board met, put me back into the system, and increased my salary to cover Social Security taxes. This would make significant financial impact later in life, for which I will be grateful to Mike Kingsbury and our board for the rest of my life.

The second provision was triggered by a substantial loss. On April 4, 2002, Suzanne's mother lost her battle with successive strokes, and we received an inheritance. Phyllis had been a generous supporter of our ministry in prayer and in finances. For the first time in our lives, we had money to invest.

We felt comfortable investing a portion of our inheritance in a pharmaceutical company, called Entropin, which was developing an arthritis-healing drug. Tom Anderson and Milt McKenzie, two of my closest friends, were principal investors. The drug had successfully passed through Phases 1 and 2 of testing; Phase 3 looked promising. Entropin had the potential to help millions of people from living in persistent pain.

Before investing, we asked ourselves, "If Entropin fails, will we lose any sleep over our financial loss?" The answer was no. That would soon be tested. In 2003, Entropin failed Phase 3. The FDA did not approve the drug, bankrupting the company. Overnight Entropin's stock became worthless; we lost our investment. We had thought this might be our golden egg, but—in the words of Milt McKenzie—"the goose didn't make it." "Well," I thought, "it looks like I will be pastoring for a long time."

We did not lose any sleep.

This is when Milt McKenzie made an offer we could not refuse. Milt was concerned about our losses. He knew I did not have an adequate retirement program—most pastors do not—so, in 2005 he invited us to invest in his privately held and extraordinarily successful oil and gas company. Oil and gas investments are notoriously risky and sometimes shady, but Milt McKenzie is a trustworthy man of great integrity. In his autobiography, *High Stakes*, Milt wrote, "I knew from an early age that relationships were more important to me than dollars and cents. As I got older, I structured my business in such a way as to build relationships with people who mattered to me."

In July 2005, we invested our savings, becoming limited partners in Milt's company. Soon an income flow began that continues to this day. In a five-year span, we went from no hope for retirement to a comfortable income—a stunning reversal. Unforeseen blessings are often associated with obeying Big Words.

Holy Discontent

My last five years at Desert Springs the congregation kept growing in depth and numbers. I started men's Bible studies and discipleship groups, which were for me fulfilling and fruitful. Staff, board, missions, and building meetings were often tedious, but a blessing because of the faithful and loving men and women.

I was becoming discontent, but it was a holy discontentment. Though at the time I didn't know it, the health and stability of the church meant it was time for me to leave. A different kind of leader was needed for Desert Spring's next stage of growth—a leader with better administrative and organizational skills.

In March 2005, the board approved a four-month sabbatical, the first of my career, from June through September. Mark Cedar, our outstanding executive pastor, oversaw the church in my absence. Suzanne and I needed time for reflection about our future. Retirement never entered our minds.

The sabbatical was broken into three parts. We started in Del Mar, California, a coastal town that we loved for its long beach walks and low-key atmosphere. This month was a planned physical, emotional, and spiritual renewal time. The second leg was two months in eastern France, in the tiny town of Sergy, across the border from Geneva, Switzerland. A former Desert Springs Church intern who became a missionary to France, asked if we would house sit for July and August while he was in the United States. The last month of the sabbatical was in Carpinteria, California, a small surfing town just south of Santa Barbara.

The month in Del Mar went as planned. Because of Mark Cedar's integrity and faithfulness, I never thought about the church; it was in capable hands. In Del Mar, God spoke to Suzanne, saying there was change coming and I would not continue as senior pastor of Desert Springs Church. God didn't tell me what she was hearing, and neither did Suzanne until we got to France.

When we boarded the plane for France, I was thoroughly relaxed and smiling. Suzanne was particularly happy; she was headed to her second home, having attended university in Strasbourg. There are no beaches in Sergy, but there are sweeping wheat, corn, and sunflower fields. Every morning we were awakened by the clip-clop of a horse being walked by a local farmer to a field down the street. After coffee and croissants, we took morning walk-talk-prayer rambles in what felt like a Vincent van Gogh painting. We also hiked in the Jura Mountains, tasted Alsatian Riesling on the Route des Vins, cheered Lance Armstrong in Paris as he dashed down the Champs-Elysees to Tour de France victory, spent a night on Mont-Saint-Michel, and toured the beaches of Normandy and the American Cemetery and Memorial.

After only two weeks in Sergy, Suzanne said, "You look like an entirely different person. I haven't seen you this relaxed and happy in years." She was right. I had developed a blood pressure condition at age fifty-two, and it all but disappeared in Sergy.

A short time later, while visiting the charming village of Kayserberg in Alsace (Albert Schweitzer's birthplace), we turned on the television in our hotel to hear the announcer say, "This is the beginning of the end of an era." Suzanne immediately sensed this was a Big Word for us—given through a television news announcer in Alsace! "A new era?" I thought. "What does that mean?"

Then on August 3, while walking through a Sergy cornfield, I told Suzanne that I had a dream in which I saw my flesh being picked at down to the bones by black birds. Ezekiel 37:1–14 immediately came to Suzanne's mind, a vision of a valley full of very dry bones. God commanded Ezekiel to prophesy life over the dry bones, and they came together, were covered with flesh, began to breathe, and became a "great army." This meant personal restoration was coming for me. New life was coming, a repurposing for a new era. She knew our time in Palm Desert was coming to an end before I did.

Later in August, while on a walk through a radiant wheat field behind our house, Suzanne asked me, "Is God speaking to you about our next ministry era? Before our sabbatical, I assumed you would pastor Desert Springs another seven years and retire at age six-ty-five. But now I'm beginning to wonder." During the sabbatical I had realized I no longer had the emotional and physical strength or desire to carry on as an effective senior pastor.

"Suzanne," I said, "I don't think I can make it to sixty-five. My brother Scott died at forty-nine, and Robin at fifty-two. If I go back and continue to serve, I think my health could deteriorate."

"Well, Kevin," she said, "you don't have to work any longer. We have the finances to retire now." In my mind, the decision was made that day in a Sergy wheat field. The Lord had spoken a Big Word.

Suzanne in a sunflower field near the town of Sergy

Careful Timing

We returned to California and to our last sabbatical month in Carpinteria. Bob and Jill Ashlock generously loaned us their second home, one block from the beach. Carpinteria was a perfect place for re-entry, and for asking one more question: "Now what?"

When God told Abram to leave Haran and "go to the land that I will show you," he did not hand him a map. Abram stepped out in faith, but he had to plan the logistics, route, and timing of his trip. Like all Big Words, Suzanne and I had to step out and step up, being careful to do everything with integrity. We needed to leave well. The process of how we resigned from Desert Springs Church was especially important.

First, we sought confirmation that we were hearing from God. I phoned my mentor, Ray Nethery, and he agreed that God was calling us to our next chapter of life. Second, I met in Aspen, Colorado, with my accountability group. Tom Anderson and Milt McKenzie wholeheartedly agreed that our tenure at Desert Springs was coming to an end. Lastly, I contacted the National Director of the Association of Vineyard Churches to arrange a meeting at our upcoming national conference in Columbus, Ohio. Unfortunately, one of his assistants cancelled five minutes before we were to meet and said it could not be rescheduled. I was disappointed but had tried my best. I did talk to the Vineyard's regional overseer, who affirmed our decision.

Significant, life-changing decisions require careful timing. Pastoral retirements can debilitate a church when made too far in advance or done too quickly. We decided to announce our decision to the church board in early January and to serve after that, if needed, no later than Easter Sunday, April 16, 2006.

We told only one staff member of our decision before January: Mark Cedar. In early October we met with Mark, who told us he had

Milt McKenzie (left) and Tom Anderson (right), loyal friends

received calls from two churches while we were on sabbatical, but he and his wife Cheri felt they were called to stay at Desert Springs Church. When we told him our plans to retire, he was stunned. But he needed to know about our plans, because we suspected the church might extend a call to him to be their next lead pastor.

We also planned a formal board and staff Christmas party at Wally's Desert Turtle, one of the finest restaurants in the Coachella Valley. Suzanne and I put a lot of thought into the evening, especially our gifts for every one of these special people. We had a great night.

When I handed my retirement letter to the board the first week in January, everyone was surprised. The church was doing well. We told them we wanted to leave behind a healthy church. They reluctantly received our announcement.

The board moved quickly, informing us that week of a generous severance package, and initiating a search for my replacement.

Immediately I became yesterday's newspaper, which is as it should be. According to our bylaws, I was recused from the process of calling a new pastor.

As I suspected, they interviewed Mark Cedar and extended a call to him. Mark met with several focus groups, answered questions in an open church forum, and after praying for several weeks, accepted the call. This was no snap decision for Mark; he too needed to hear God's voice. On April 9—a beautiful, bright desert day— Mark was installed as pastor. I had arranged a welcome luncheon at El Dorado Country Club, inviting board, church staff, and local pastors. When the luncheon was underway, Suzanne and I slipped out the back, walked past the beautifully tended bougainvillea and world class golf course. Old pastors, it turns out, quietly move on to their next assignment. God was not through with us.

My time in Palm Desert had come to an end. To what great unimagined adventure was God calling us? We needed a Big Word.

NINE

The Adventure Continues

Camarillo, California

"Calling helps us to finish well because it prevents us from confusing the termination of our occupations with the termination of our vocations."
—Os Guinness, *The Call*

For our entire married lives, Suzanne and I had always agreed on each of our geographic moves. She had never complained about any of our assignments, knowing they were God's Big Words for us in each chapter of our lives. Many of the moves, however, were initiated by job opportunities for me. But this move would be different. As I prayed about our new assignment, the Lord said, "Let Suzanne choose where to live."

Although this was her decision, I voiced my opinion. I preferred to move to Carpinteria, a perfect place to retire as a beach bum. I even knew specifically where I wanted to live: a studio condominium near the beach. I'd stack my surf boards outside the front door, wear jams surf shorts, and enjoy Pacific Ocean sunsets for the rest of my life. My retirement goals were not high. In my last message to Desert Springs Church, I said, "I'm not leaving you for another church. I will never be a lead pastor again." This didn't mean that I did not have high goals for retirement. But at the age of 58, I was fulfilled but worn out, which contributed to thinking retirement meant an extended vacation.

I, I, I; me, me, me. This was all about me.

When exhausted, hearing God's voice is difficult. Back in the ninth century B.C., after faithfully serving God, the prophet Elijah hit an emotional, spiritual, and physical wall. His story is found in 1 Kings 18–19. Elijah fought many battles, culminating in an intense conflict at Mt. Carmel with the evil and idolatrous King Ahab and his murderous pagan wife Jezebel. That day he defeated—slaughtered—450 prophets of Baal but hit a tipping point when Jezebel threatened his life. Elijah snapped, fearfully running away into the wilderness. There he begged God to take his life. Instead, God dispatched an angel to minister to him with food and drink, fortifying him for a walk of forty days and nights to Horeb, the mount of God, where Elijah hid in a cave.

Then God came to Elijah, asking, "What are you doing here, Elijah?" Elijah whined, "I have been very jealous for the Lord, the God of hosts . . . I, even I only am left, and they seek my life, to take it away." Elijah suffered from a bad case of warped thinking; God informed him seven thousand in Israel had not bowed to Baal. After bellyaching to God about the difficulty of obeying Big Words, the Lord spoke to Elijah in a soft voice, directing him to anoint new kings and a new prophet—Elisha—who eventually would replace him. Elijah obeyed and ministered with Elisha, who encouraged and strengthened him. God was not through with Elijah.

Like Elijah, I wanted to live in a cave—my cave was Carpinteria. Looking back on this time, I think I suffered from a post-retirement let-down. My prayers were more weary complaints than joyful gratitude. Leaders in all walks of life take many body blows: attacks, disappointments, rejections, and setbacks. This goes with the territory. With each defeat most leaders get up and keep moving forward—but are a little weaker if not wiser. When Elijah withdrew, God understood. He sent an angel to strengthen him. Then he spoke to him. "Here's your next mission. Now, get up and get on with it." God did the same for me.

In one sense, there is no retirement for Christians. Paul wrote, regarding the nation of Israel, "the gifts and the calling of God are irrevocable" (Romans 11:29). This truth applies to everyone who turns to God. My unique gifts and calling *are* irrevocable. Once Big Words are fulfilled, God gives new assignments. "So even to old age and gray hairs, O God, do not forsake me," the writer of Psalm 71 prays, "until I proclaim your might to another generation, your power to all those to come." Roles may change, but the calling remains the same.

In another sense, there *is* retirement for Christians—not a retirement from serving God but a reassignment to serve in more supportive roles. In the Old Testament, God instructed the Levites—those who ministered in the Holy Temple—to serve from the age of twenty-five "and from the age of fifty years they shall withdraw from the duty of service and serve no more." But God was not finished with the Levites. He said, "They minister to their brothers in the tent of meeting by keeping guard . . ." (Numbers 8:23–26). They were called to encourage, warn, coach, pray for, listen to, protect . . . to do anything to help their younger brothers faithfully fulfill their Levitical duties.

Our Big Word from Isaiah 43:19 had been fulfilled in Palm Desert. I withdrew from my duty of service at Desert Springs. I too was called to encourage, warn, coach, pray for, listen to, protect—anything to help younger brothers and sisters to faithfully fulfill their high callings. To paraphrase Os Guinness, termination of my occupation was not the cancellation of my vocation.

I was *not* called to be a surf bum in Carpinteria.

Committed to Others' Success

Suzanne was confident that God was not through with us. She never saw retirement as a vacation from serving God and others. In fact, Suzanne did not like the word retirement. "God is going to use our gifts and experience for a new stage of life! He's going to repurpose us. We must keep on keeping on. Springers don't quit."

That, in a nutshell, was God's Big Word for the next leg of our journey: "God is going to repurpose us. *Finish well.*"

Suzanne chose the city of Camarillo, so off we went! Psalm 139:3 says, "You chart the path ahead of me and tell me where to stop and rest. Every moment you know where I am" (TLB).

One hundred eighty miles west of Palm Desert, Camarillo is situated on the fertile Oxnard Plain near the Pacific Ocean in Ventura County. Camarillo features a Mediterranean climate, proximity to the beach, delectable strawberries, and easy access to Santa Barbara, Malibu, and Los Angeles. But for Suzanne and me those attributes paled in comparison to one allure: Grandchildren. Annie, our granddaughter, and grandson J.D. lived in Camarillo. A significant portion of the next chapter in life would focus on family.

Camarillo, the home of grandchildren (top left, clockwise) J.D., Annie, Micah, Benjamin and Titus

Divine Healing

The first two years of retirement were about restoration and renewal. Shortly after our oldest daughter Kelley bought a condominium in Camarillo, she was offered a teaching position at the American School in Paris, France. We were not ready to buy a new home, so renting her condo made an easy transition for us and a worry-free move for Kelley. The condominium was also near our other daughter's family.

Life was going smoothly until early 2008 when Suzanne developed health problems, necessitating an operation on February 4. Complications resulted. Her left ureter was blocked, a serious condition which two ensuing procedures failed to correct. For six weeks she wore a nephrostomy bag with a tube inserted through her back into her left kidney. This was a challenging time of doctors' appointments, painful recovery, uncertainty, and much prayer. Living for God doesn't exempt us from the vicissitudes of life.

Finally, the decision was made to operate yet again. On Monday, March 24, the day after Easter, we drove to Reseda for a three-to-four-hour operation. Before Suzanne was wheeled on a gurney into the operating room, I laid hands on her and prayed again for healing. Her outstanding surgeon, Joseph Navon, was Jewish, so Suzanne quoted to him from Psalm 91—"He who dwells in the shelter of the Most High will abide in the shadow of the Almighty"—before being anesthetized.

Waiting downstairs with our youngest daughter Alyssa, I nervously paced outside the front doors while I prayed. Only sixty minutes after the operation began, I was startled by Dr. Navon walking up to me. With a big smile he said, "Don't worry, Kevin. Everything is all right. It's an Easter miracle." He then described how with scalpel in hand preparing to cut open Suzanne's abdomen, he noticed something was wrong. Or rather something was right. So, he put the scalpel down, ran a test, and discovered the ureter was open and functioning as it should be. Suzanne was healed. "I have never had something like this happen before." Unknown to us, our friend Wanda Levine and Suzanne's brother, Jim, individually had specifically prayed for a creative miracle. Their prayers, those of many others, and mine were answered.

Suzanne awakened in recovery to hear her non-operation was a complete success. God had healed her! Her response? She thanked Christ and said, "I'm really hungry. Can we eat at Marmalade Cafe in Westlake Village?" Off we went, celebrating her healing all the way down the Ventura Freeway to the cafe. After being seated, a young waitress approached our table and asked, "What are you so happy about?" Suzanne blurted out, "God healed my ureter! Do you know what a ureter is?"

The waitress teared up, saying, "My entire life I've suffered with defective ureters. I've been in and out of urologists' offices

with no success. They don't know what to do. I'm so discouraged."
Suzanne prayed for her, and she ran off to tell the other waitresses,
"Come and see the woman whose ureter God healed!" Blessings
are meant to be shared with others.

After Suzanne's healing, I started accepting preaching invita-
tions and building coaching relationships with younger pastors. To
use a baseball analogy, I was now a utility player on God's team—
serving in a variety of roles to encourage younger pastors. I liked
this part of my journey because I love seeing others succeed.

San Luis Obispo

In June 2008, Kelley returned home from Paris, and we rented a
home in Old Town Camarillo. Enjoying the community feel of Old
Town, we thought one day we would like to own in this neighborhood—though we still did not have peace about buying in an
unstable and inflated housing market.

In September, Thom O'Leary, pastor of Mountainbrook Church
in San Luis Obispo, approached me about coming on staff part-
time to help his church transition from a rented warehouse to a
building on a spectacular sixty-three-acre site overlooking the city.
The leadership challenges of such a move were monumental. Tom
and I had annually swapped pulpits for years; he looked to me as
a mentor. Suzanne and I knew and loved Mountainbrook Church,
so I accepted a position that necessitated commuting 140 miles up
the coast from Camarillo for two or three days every week or two.
I slept in Tom and Sherri's guest house, nestled in the picturesque
Edna Valley Vineyard, known for their chardonnays. For three years
I preached occasionally, led the men's ministry, worked with small
groups, and encouraged Tom as he made significant staffing and
financial decisions. I love, respect, and appreciate Thom and Sherri.

Other assignments followed. In September of 2011, shortly after I finished serving Mountainbrook Church, executive pastor Dan Miller invited me to be part-time staff at Living Oaks Church in nearby Newbury Park, where I served for three years. I continued accepting speaking engagements, and maintained relationships with pastoral leaders—praying, mentoring, encouraging, listening.

By the fall of 2010, we were ready to buy a home in Old Town. On October 29, a home we loved became available, then owned by Wells Fargo Bank. We had one day to make an offer, and the offer was accepted; we received the keys to our new home on December 23. After extensive painting and some renovations, we moved in on February 6, 2011. Because we purchased after the housing market crashed, we paid $334,000 below what it sold for five years earlier. God's timing was magnificent.

Perhaps the most significant feature of our home is a cozy casita (Spanish for little house), which we dedicated to God to host pastors, missionaries, friends, or folks who were in transition or hurting. Hospitality is in our spiritual DNA, a prominent feature of Suzanne's gift mix. God provided a home so we could serve our family and others. Over the years, numerous pastoral leaders and people in need or transition have stayed in our guest house. Ministry now regularly comes to our home.

The Good Fight

On Friday, June 4, 2010, John Hartfield, a lay pastor, good friend, and golfing buddy from Palm Desert, visited for a couple of days. Suzanne was away with her sister, so this was an ideal time to renew our relationship. When John and I had first met, we instantly bonded, perhaps because we were "cheese heads"—both born in Wisconsin. We dreamed of sitting together at a Rose Bowl game in

Pasadena on January 1, watching Wisconsin and USC battle it out on the gridiron.

John was seventy years old, but he looked younger. A former Division 1 scholarship athlete at the University of Wisconsin, he was strapping at six-foot-two and could still hit a golf ball. The Saturday of his visit, John shot a 73 at the Buenaventura Golf Course. What I remember most about that round of golf was his sharing the gospel with two young men who were paired with us. John could not stop talking about his relationship with Christ. His life verse was 2 Timothy 4:7, "I have fought the good fight, I have finished the race, and I have remained faithful." He was fighting "*the* good fight," not "*a* good fight"—the significant fight, being an ambassador of the good news that Christ died for our sins. "I didn't start out life well," he would tell me, "but I'm determined to finish well." John was not going to let his past determine his future.

When John and Sandra, his wife, had started attending Desert Springs ten years earlier, they had a profound encounter with Christ. John's spiritual heart was set on fire, enlarged by the Holy Spirit. His nickname from college days was, prophetically, Hartsy, which is paradoxical, because John literally had a small heart due to a genetic anomaly. John had internal organs the size of a twelve-year-old boy. This created serious, on-going heart ailments, first appearing at age forty. He frequently needed to go to Scripps Memorial Hospital in La Jolla.

The World's Best Intern

John understood hospitals and suffering, so I had asked him if he would like to be trained as Desert Springs pastor of hospital visitation. He jumped at the opportunity. I have never known a more effective and compassionate minister to the sick and hurting than John.

I started calling him "The World's Oldest Intern Pastor," a title he proudly accepted; he was soon recognized as a pastor in our church.

After playing our round of golf that Saturday in Ventura, he said, "Kevin, I want to buy you a good steak dinner. I've got something to tell you about my latest visit to Scripps." I suspected he had bad news about his small physical heart. I was wrong. "I've been diagnosed with advanced pancreatic cancer, though I don't feel sick yet. I need to go in for a tricky surgery at the University of California at Irvine on July 21. I think it's a Hail Mary, because the doctors encouraged me to take Sandra on a special vacation before then, so we're going on an Alaskan cruise."

Since many members of his family were planning to be at the hospital the day of the operation, we agreed it would be better for him if I came the following day. However, the morning of the operation I received a tearful call from Sandra, informing me the operation did not go well. "Could you come to the hospital right now?" Two hours later I was meeting with Sandra and John's surgeon.

The surgeon was shaken. "His organs are so unusually small we could not reconnect the blood supply to his intestines."

"What does that mean?"

Responding ominously, "Well, we need to run more tests." Sandra left the room in tears, leaving me alone with the surgeon.

"Doctor, will the tests change the prognosis?"

"No. With no blood supply to his intestines, John will die within twenty-four hours. A palliative physician will oversee his last hours. The pain of dying this way is profound. This evening John will be put into a coma, never to awaken again. This is necessary for his comfort. He will not feel any pain."

By now John was out of recovery and back in his room. Sandra decided I should be there when he was told by the surgeon that he had at most twenty-four hours to live. I was his friend and pastor; this was fitting and proper. He was feeling good and quite alert when I walked into the room. He asked, "Is it finished?" I responded, "Yes, John, the operation is finished." "No," John said, "I mean, am I finished? I think I'm finished." Somehow, he knew his time was up, even though the surgeon wasn't to tell him for a few minutes.

The palliative doctor was a Christian, reassuring him it was for his good that he be put in a medically induced coma early that evening, and that he was not hastening his death. "The next time you are conscious," this wonderful doctor reassured him, "you will be in the presence of Christ."

But the good race was not yet over for John Hartfield. After we prayed, he asked for his well-worn Bible and called his family members into the room. I faded to the background, and just before he started sharing the gospel from the book of Romans to the packed room, I waved goodbye to John and said, "Well, the next time we see each other will be in heaven." He responded, "It'll be sooner than you think."

The next morning, John Hartfield died. He had the hope of heaven. He finished well.

The Race

The Apostle Paul was dedicated to finishing well, comparing life to a race in which the winner arrives at the finish line having completed his high calling. "I consider my life worth nothing to me," he said, adding "my only aim is to finish the race and complete that task the Lord Jesus has given me—the task of testifying to the good news of God's grace" (Acts 20:24, NIV). The way into a relationship with Christ—by grace, through faith—is the way to complete our high calling. This race is more a marathon than a sprint.

Why did Paul and my friend John Hartfield succeed where so many have failed? Many believers who start well do not finish well, falling short of their high calling. Why? They have not discovered the challenges to finishing well.

During her junior year of high school, I attended my grand-daughter Annie's league championship race in cross country. She had trained hard year-round and felt good going into the finals. The three-mile course began on a flat, grassy park, descending into a ravine on a narrow dirt path before winding through some woods, under a bridge, more woods, then ascending back to the open park and the finish line. In most meets, Annie was her team's fastest runner, but in this race calamity struck. After passing under the bridge Annie was leading her team when another runner clipped her heel from behind and she fell hard, ripping a gash in her right leg. Stunned and bleeding, Annie pulled herself together and pursued the pack for the longest two miles of her cross-country career. Quitting and pain never entered her mind. "I can do all things through Christ," she kept saying to herself, "who strengthens me." She concentrated on passing girls ahead of her while focusing on the finish line and winning a league medal. Over the last mile she picked up her pace while teammates, coaches, friends, and family cheered her on, placing second for her team and in the league's top ten finishers, earning her a medal. I have never been prouder of Annie than that day. She finished the race well.

Annie's story is a parable containing four challenges of how to finish life well, which are found in Hebrews 12:1–2:

> Therefore, since we are surrounded by so great a cloud of witnesses, let us also lay aside every weight, and sin which clings so closely, and let us run with endurance the race that is set before

us, looking to Jesus, the founder and perfecter of our faith, who for the joy that was set before him endured the cross, despising the shame, and is seated at the right hand of the throne of God.

The Great Cloud of Witnesses

The first challenge to finishing well is staying connected with family, friends, mentors, mentees, and the examples of saints found in Scripture and church history—the "great cloud of witnesses" mentioned in Hebrews 12:1. Isolation is a tool of the enemy. We have been created for relationships. Annie's coaches, family, team-mates, and friends made the difference at the end of her race, cheering her through the most challenging part—the last 400 meters.

My "great cloud of witnesses" is extensive, beginning with Suzanne and our parents, our children and their spouses, and grandchildren (Annie, J.D., Micah, Titus, and Benjamin); then expanding in concentric circles from mentors like Ray Nethery and John Wimber; teachers and professors like Jon Braun and Joe Kickasola; life-long friends like Tom and Maggie LePley; special-ized mentors like Kevin Perrotta; contemporary theologians and thinkers like Wayne Grudem and Os Guinness; supporters like Milt McKenzie and Tom Anderson; colleagues and trusted brothers like Keith Newsome and Dave Nodar; older brothers like Jack Bailey and George Henderson; writers like C. S. Lewis, Francis Schaeffer, Henri J. M. Nouwen, Dallas Willard, and Timothy Keller; historical fathers of the faith like Augustine and Calvin; and last though not least, the pastors of my church, Soli Deo Gloria. I dare not forget Billy Graham, who preached the gospel the day God extended a personal invitation to me to be God's adopted son. Dr. Graham finished well. Many on the list of giants of the faith found in Hebrews 11—men and women like Noah, Abraham and Sarah,

Isaac, Moses, Rahab, Samson, David—were imperfect, but when they slipped, they got up and kept moving toward God. My list, of course, is a sampler; there are many more in my life. Without them, I could not finish well.

Granddaughter Annie West, finishing well

Carrying Extra Weight

The second challenge to finishing well is letting go of personal baggage that weighs us down "and sin which clings so closely" (Hebrews 12:1). Annie finished her race well because she trained hard and was not carrying excess weight, the bane of all distance runners. The "weight" referred to by the writer of Hebrews is residual emotional issues and sins carrying hurt, pain, sadness, regret, and even anger. When left unresolved, pent-up emotional issues and unconfessed sin are detrimental to our physical, emotional, spiritual, and mental health. I've dealt with many kinds of personal baggage: resentments and grudges; jealousies and insecurities; disappointments, failures, and regrets. The list is long.

Toward the end of our lives, these problems left unresolved linger, forming a web of deceit that holds us back from moving forward. There is only one way out: repentance and faith. One of my life Scriptures has helped me here, Ephesians 2:8–9, "By grace you have been saved through faith. And this is not your own doing; it is the gift of God, not a result of works, so that no one may boast."

God's grace, Jesus' dying for my sins, is the basis for my forgiveness. Grace is his love, undeserved and unearned by me, extended freely through his eternal sacrifice, resurrection, and ascension. After reminding me "your Father knows exactly what you need even before you ask him," Jesus taught me to pray "forgive us our sins, as we have forgiven those who sin against us" (Matthew 6:8, 12 NLT). I am forgiven so I can forgive others. To drive this point home, after teaching the disciples how to pray, Jesus adds, "If you forgive those who sin against you, your heavenly Father will forgive you. But if you refuse to forgive others, your Father will not forgive your sins" (Matthew 6:14–15, NLT).

When I look in the mirror and see the sin that clings to me, I try to remember that my short-comings and failures qualify me for his grace. For me there is no better reminder of God's grace than the sacrament of Communion—participation in the body and blood of Christ. Worship, repentance and forgiveness, listening to God's word, confessing our faith, and receiving the reminders of his grace are a tremendous way to begin every week.

God's grace is not an excuse to continue sinning with impunity; grace gives me freedom to pursue a higher purpose: "For we are his [God's] workmanship, created in Christ Jesus for good works, which *God prepared beforehand, that we should walk in them*" (Ephesians 2:10).

Strength Under Control

The third challenge to finishing well is running "with endurance the race that is set before us." Annie's cross-country race again illustrates this well. The word translated endurance means patience, steadfastness, perseverance. Runners who finish well know how to set a strategic and patient pace, reserving energy for climbing mountains and a strong kick near the finish. Annie got up and ran to finish the race. She didn't panic when she fell. She ran hard, but she ran smart. Many believers burn out at the beginning of their journey with Christ, so when they hit life's challenges, they drop out.

The Finish Line

This leads to the last challenge of finishing well: focusing on the finish line, the goal. Look "to Jesus, the founder and perfecter of our faith, who for the joy that was set before him endured the cross, despising the shame, and is seated at the right hand of the throne of God" (Hebrews 12:2). If I don't know where I am going, any old path will take me there. But I run "the race that is set before [me]." I can be surrounded with empowering, supportive relationships, honestly deal with the sin and burdens that weigh me down, and run with endurance, but if I fail to run the unique, narrow path that God has set out, I am lost. Annie has run in races where girls did not finish well because they wandered off the path, failing to look for course markings at confusing forks in the road. I too will miss the path that God marked out for me if I'm not listening to God's voice and following his Big Words, his unique path markers.

Seeing the prize at end of the race—the presence of Christ—provides strength and encouragement through the setbacks and discouragement of life. But what does that end look like?

In February 2012, four years after Suzanne's healing, I was diagnosed with skin cancer on my face. I thought, "Wouldn't it be great if I had a *new* body?" There is a yearning common to all men and women for new beginnings: a new body; new home; new job; new car; new start. We want freedom from something—from debt or depression; anxiety or addiction; broken relationships or bitterness; guilt or grief; from sickness or sadness; from despair or death—ultimately from our own death.

We must admit that intuitively we know that we were created for more than even the best of what this world offers. My body is as brief as a vapor and as fragile as a butterfly wing. The poet Carl Sandburg succinctly described life as: "Born-Troubled-Died." Surely there is more to our existence than this life.

Yearning for an eternity free from the ravages of death is common to people everywhere and for all time. That is what Abraham was looking for when in obedience to God he and Sarah left Haran, traveling 600 miles to Canaan:

> By faith Abraham obeyed when he was called to go out to a place that he was to receive as an inheritance. And he went out, not knowing where he was going. . . . For he was looking forward to the city that has foundations, whose designer and builder is God. **(Hebrews 11:8, 10)**

Abraham and Sarah were looking for a different kind of world, one free from suffering, hatred, and death. They sought a city whose architect and builder was God himself. That is what God had promised them. But neither Abraham nor any of the "heroes of faith" mentioned in Hebrews 11 entered that eternal city!

> These all died in faith, not having received the things promised,
> but having seen them and greeted them from afar, and having
> acknowledged that they were strangers and exiles on the earth...
> But as it is, they desire a better country, that is, a heavenly one.
> Therefore, God is not ashamed to be called their God, for he has
> prepared for them a city. **(Hebrews 11:13, 16)**

I may be in this world, but I am not of this world. A stranger
and exile in a foreign land, I yearn for a world freed from decay and
death. I am part of a different breed, the brotherhood and sisterhood
of the redeemed in Christ. The apostle John wrote, "Do not love the
world or the things in the world" (1 John 2:15). By "world" John
refers not to creation but to "the desires of the flesh and the desires
of the eyes and pride of life" (1 John 2:16). My high calling keeps
me journeying with purpose; the destination—the new heaven and
earth—keeps me persevering with hope. "Our heavenly Father
has provided many delightful inns for us along our journey," C. S.
Lewis wrote, "but he takes great care to see that we do not mistake
any of them for home."

Because I know my destiny, I am free to live the most radical
life of love and sacrifice here on earth. Knowing where I am going
means living fully in the moment with the hope of eternity in view.

The New Jerusalem

I thought I might be facing death when my outstanding dermatolo-
gist diagnosed melanoma, pending a pathologist's confirmation of
my biopsy. He referred me to a surgeon who also said it looked like
cancer and recommended surgery as soon as possible. My older
brother, Robin, died from melanoma at age fifty-two. Yet I peace-
fully received the diagnosis, telling both doctors I didn't fear death

because I knew Christ. Admittedly, I was anxious about the *process* of dying, but not my ultimate destination, which is described by John in Revelation 21:1–5:

> Then I saw a new heaven and a new earth, for the first heaven and the first earth had passed away, and the sea was no more. And I saw the holy city, new Jerusalem, coming down out of heaven from God, prepared as a bride adorned for her husband. And I heard a loud voice from the throne saying, "Behold, the dwelling place of God is with man. He will dwell with them, and they will be his people, and God himself will be with them as their God. He will wipe away every tear from their eyes, and death shall be no more, neither shall there be mourning, nor crying, nor pain anymore, for the former things have passed away." And he who was seated on the throne said, "Behold, I am making all things new."

One word stands out in this passage: "new," found four times. God's ultimate purpose for humanity and creation is unfulfilled until he makes all things new. But what exactly is God's newness? John, the writer of Revelation, chose a specific Greek word that we translate into English "new," meaning new in quality, freshness, brightness, and strength, as in substantially better and superior to the old. To quote Timothy Keller, "The Ancient of Ancients is new and everything he touches is new. In God everything becomes newer and newer; fresher and fresher; brighter and brighter; more whole; more beautiful every second." He makes everything new, and then continues to renew.

The Bible does not teach that after death we will live for eternity as disembodied spirits, free from our physical bodies. God will not say good riddance to our physical bodies. At Christ's return, our bodies will be glorified like his resurrected body. "Our citizenship is in heaven," Paul says, "and from it we await a Savior, the Lord Jesus Christ, who will transform our lowly body to be like his glorious body" (Philippians 3:20–21). Our bodies will be made new. No more tears. No more pain. No more death. No more cancer.

Andrew Peterson captures my longing for newness well in his hymn, *Is He Worthy?*

> *Do you feel the world is broken? (We do)*
> *Do you feel the shadows deepen? (We do)*
> *But do you know that all the dark won't stop*
> *The light from getting through? (We do)*
> *Do you wish that you could see it all made new? (We do)*
>
> *Is all creation groaning? (It is)*
> *Is a new creation coming? (It is)*
> *Is the glory of the Lord to be the light within our midst? (It is)*
> *Is it good that we remind ourselves of this? (It is)*

I would be remiss if I didn't tell the rest of my cancer story, because it had a happy ending. It turned out that either there was a premature diagnosis needing confirmation or after a correct diagnosis there was a divine healing, one that the doctors would not believe until conducting three biopsies, all of which came back benign. One pathologist even called my doctor, asking, "Who is this Kevin Springer?" A small biopsy scar just below the left side of my lip reminds me of God's grace every morning while brushing my teeth. I am officially cancer free. I like to say I was healed from my non-cancer. I will live to die another day.

Hope

In his book, *Man's Search for Meaning*, holocaust survivor Viktor Frankl writes about the record death rate in Auschwitz between Christmas 1944 and January 1945. The inmates died, he says, because they had expected to be home by Christmas; when they realized they would not return, they lost hope of ever escaping imprisonment and gave up trying. Hope also is a critical component to finishing well. Paul, in commending the Colossian Christians for their faith in Christ and love for others, said that was "because of the hope laid up for [them] in heaven" (Colossians 1:5).

When John Hartfield was told he only had twenty-four hours to live, he asked for his Bible and preached the good news of hope to a packed hospital room. He said that Christ died so death and fear would no longer enslave us. John had a smile on his face as I left his room, because he knew he would shortly be with the Creator and Savior of the world, Jesus Christ. "Hope," G. K. Chesterton wrote, "means hoping when everything seems hopeless." As agents of hope, our witness shines most powerfully in despairing circumstances. That motivates me for finishing well.

The New Jerusalem, our final destination, is the promise of what Christ brought in his first coming—the future invading the present, hope defeating despair, meaning overcoming nihilism, new life conquering death. "Easter," N. T. Wright says, "was when Hope in person surprised the whole world by coming forward from the future to the present."

Today, I experience hors d'oeuvres of the fulness of eternity future, foretastes of the Marriage Supper of the Lamb described in Revelation 19. Every Lord's Day, when participating in the sacrament of communion, I am rehearsing a dinner in the new heaven and earth. The meal reminds me of my forgiveness, which makes possible intimacy with my heavenly Father as his adopted son. I confess my faith with brothers and sisters and experience the empowering and leading of the Holy Spirit. I hear God's voice spoken from the Scriptures and also preached. These little tastes, down payments of hope, provide the courage to finish well and fulfill my unimagined adventure with God.

Soli Deo Gloria. To God alone be the glory.

The Springer Family,
Our 50th Anniversary, March 29, 2019, Santa Barbara, California

What's Your Unimagined Adventure?

Camarillo, California

"Only a very hardy individualist or social rebel—or one desperate for another life—stands any chance of discovering the substantiality of the spiritual life today."
—Dallas Willard, *Hearing God: Developing a Conversational Relationship with God*

A *Road of Unimagined Adventure* is a bridge over "a chasm vast and deep and wide... through which was flowing a sullen tide," in poet Will Allen Dromgoole's words, that separates post-modern people from hearing God's voice. This journey invites everyone to Christ's supernatural friendship.

But what is that chasm that must be crossed "in the twilight dim"? For many people, the sullen tide is a polarized culture, divided between religion and science. One side believes there is a Creator who has redeemed his broken world; the other believes men and women can trust only their five senses.

These two worldviews wrestle in the hearts and minds of men and women. Science is labeled as fact and reality, religion as subjective and mere opinion. Philosophy professor Dallas Willard wrote, "Students in our colleges and universities live constantly in a tension between two authority systems: one more or less vaguely associated with science and the other with religion." Willard tells the story of a conversation between one of his students and a physics professor in which the student mentioned the bodily resurrection of Christ, and the physics professor responded, "The resurrection is inconsistent with the laws of physics." In other words, dead men don't rise; therefore, the resurrection of Christ—*the* central tenet of Christianity—is dismissed.

This elevation of science as the superior if not exclusive source of truth and reality is called scientism. Christian philosopher and theologian J. P. Moreland writes:

> *Roughly, scientism is the view that the hard sciences—like chemistry, biology, physics, astronomy—provide the only genuine knowledge of reality. At the very least, this scientific knowledge is vastly superior to what we can know from any other discipline.*

Moreland concludes, "As the ideas that constitute scientism have become more pervasive in our culture, the Western world has… come increasingly to regard religion as a private superstition."

You may be sympathetic to this view of truth, agreeing with the Hungarian-American psychiatrist Thomas Szasz who wrote, "If you talk to God, you are praying; if God talks to you, you have schizophrenia."

A Road of Unimagined Adventure, however, contends these two authority systems—science (*not* scientism) and faith—coexist without impugning each other. God does not call us to choose either/or but both/and. No less than Albert Einstein wrote, "It would be possible to describe everything scientifically, but it would make no sense; it would be without meaning, as if you described a Beethoven symphony as a variation of wave pressure." That is a both/and statement.

Science fails to answer many of life's transcendent questions: What is the basis for moral truth? Am I really living or merely surviving? What are the qualities of a profoundly good life? How do I become a good person? Do humans have souls? What happens after death?

I think of my life more as a ballet than an algorithm—faith and science are friends, not foes, and the object of my faith, Jesus Christ, gives meaning to everything that happens around me and to me. Indeed, the idea that God would create an orderly universe with properties that can be rationally understood, is a long-held Christian belief. Many of the great scientists in history were Christians, including the godfathers of modern science: Isaac Newton, Galileo, Johannes Kepler, Nicolaus Copernicus. In college, I never felt a tension between my biological studies and my faith. Science was a way of knowing more about God for me.

So, if there is a God who created and sustains an orderly, rational world, it stands to reason that he can and does break into it—as its Creator this is his prerogative. But can you experience him as I describe in this book? Intimately? Profoundly? Authoritatively? Are my Big Words the testimony of a schizophrenic, or the witness of someone who genuinely knows God? That is for you to decide, but the only rational (and honest) way to know, is to ask the Big Question, "God, if you are there, will you show yourself to me?"

Why not you? Why don't you ask God for Big Words, then—when he speaks—step out in faith and see if they shape your life? If you take the challenge, most likely you fall into the category of "hardy individualist, social rebel, or desperate for another type of life"—it matters not to God—he just wants to show you his love and care. He wants you to hear his voice, to experience a genuinely spiritual life.

Why not consciously cultivate a listening heart and mind to receive God's Big Words? I suggest that you start with King David's prayer in Psalm 28:1.

> To you, O Lord, I call;
> My rock, be not deaf to me,
> Lest, if you be silent to me,
> I become like those who go down to the pit.

A Road of Unimagined Adventure is my story of the normal Christian life. This can be your story too—if you let God direct an adventure uniquely fitted to you.

What's your unimagined adventure?

ABOUT THE AUTHOR

Kevin Noble Springer is a retired pastor of the Desert Springs Church in Palm Desert, California, magazine editor, and author of numerous books and articles published in multiple languages. In 2006, *Power Evangelism*, cowritten with John Wimber, was named the twelfth most significant book in evangelical Christianity in the past fifty years by *Christianity Today*. His other titles with John Wimber include *Power Healing*, and *Power Points*. He also wrote *The Way to Maturity* and *The Kingdom and the Power*, co-edited with Gary S. Greig. Kevin is married to Suzanne Nadal, his wife of over five decades, with whom he has conducted marriage seminars in North America and Europe. They live in Camarillo, California, near their three married children and five grandchildren. Kevin earned a B.S. in Biology from the University of Southern California and an M.A. in Theology from Ashland (Ohio) Theological Seminary.

A free ebook edition is available with the purchase of this book.

To claim your free ebook edition:

1. Visit MorganJamesBOGO.com
2. Sign your name CLEARLY in the space
3. Complete the form and submit a photo of the entire copyright page
4. You or your friend can download the ebook to your preferred device

Morgan James
BOGO™

A **FREE** ebook edition is available for you
or a friend with the purchase of this print book.

CLEARLY SIGN YOUR NAME ABOVE

Instructions to claim your free ebook edition:
1. Visit MorganJamesBOGO.com
2. Sign your name CLEARLY in the space above
3. Complete the form and submit a photo
   of this entire page
4. You or your friend can download the ebook
   to your preferred device

Print & Digital Together Forever.

Snap a photo

Free ebook

Read anywhere